HUMAN RESOURCES STRATEGIES IN ASIA

HOW TO CREATE A COMPETITIVE EDGE

HOWARD CANT

MINERVA PRESS
LONDON WASHINGTON

HUMAN RESOURCES STRATEGIES IN ASIA
HOW TO CREATE A COMPETITIVE EDGE

Copyright Howard Cant © 1994

ISBN 1 85863 118 1

First Published 1994 by
MINERVA PRESS
2, Old Brompton Road,
London SW7 3DQ.

Printed in Great Britain by
Antony Rowe., Chippenham, Wiltshire.

HUMAN RESOURCE STRATEGIES IN ASIA

HOW TO CREATE A COMPETITIVE EDGE

Howard Cant

Howard Cant is a consultant currently focusing on how Human Resources strategies create a competitive advantage in business. He has over twenty years experience with multi-national companies in General and Human Resources Management, the last twelve of which have been spent in Asia.

He is the Managing Director of "Ingram Associates" a Human Resources and Organisational Improvement consultancy, it's headquarters being located in Singapore.

CB EO

*To my
Mother and Father,
Bob and Betty Cant
with love.*

CB EO

CONTENTS

**HUMAN RESOURCES STRATEGIES IN ASIA -
HOW TO CREATE A COMPETITIVE EDGE**

CHAPTER 1
THE CHANGING PROFILE OF
HUMAN RESOURCES IN ASIA

Until recent times, the idea of including the Director of Human Resources, assuming the position existed at all, in discussions on the strategic direction of a company in Asia, would have been unusual. Only the most forward thinking companies and those usually with a strong connection to a multi-national operation would contemplate such a step. This is because Asia has largely been seen as a window of opportunity for entrepreneurial Western companies, for family owned national conglomerates and aggressive but, paradoxically, patient Japanese businessmen. These three types of marketers characteristically allowed themselves little time for concern with the retention and development of staff, often viewing this element of their business as little more than a necessary high cost mechanism to penetrate new markets with innovative products.

But the times and tides in Asia are changing. Skilled entrepreneurial and managerial talent in Asia now sits very securely in the "seller's" chair with an ability to demand not only considerable compensation and benefits packages but also an increasingly loud voice in the functioning and future development of their companies and of themselves. Management is forced to sit up and take notice as they recognise that their real competitive edge is the quality and loyalty of their people. Everyone has access to the same markets. Product quality, because of excellent marketing methods and the welcoming grip of total quality management, just-in-time and continuous improvement techniques, offers little differentiation from one company to another. The only really definable and enduring difference is the quality level, commitment and enthusiasm of employees. Improved results in business today come primarily from the employee's motivational drive to offer their employers enhanced added-value. The important business question then becomes, how do we ensure the retention and development of this commitment to added value by our staff?

In essence, how can we ensure that the management of our human resources is understood from the top of the organisation to the bottom to be one of essential strategic importance to our company? And, having ensured this, how do our policies in this area of management create a competitive advantage for us? These are the major management questions in Asia today and for the next decade.

Industrial history in Asia is short with one or two notable exceptions. When one remembers that China, Thailand and Indonesia have an industrialisation process of little more than fifteen years and that, at the other end of the scale, Japan, Australia and India have considerably less than one hundred years, perhaps even less than fifty years, we begin to understand some of the dimensions of the remarkable modernisation process occurring today in Asia and the severe growing pains accompanying it. Overheated China with more than one thousand million people achieving an economic growth rate of ten per cent per year and requiring ten million managers to be trained in basic business techniques before they can begin to become effective, is perhaps the most difficult problem to solve. Japan's and Australia's recessions show another piece of the huge jigsaw of Asia which lacks basic earth and sky parts in one region and has too many in another.

The newest industrialised Asian countries lack skills in most areas notably engineering, middle and senior management. Huge Indonesian conglomerates are being run by ambitious, hard-working and capable young men who, despite their enthusiasm, lack many of the worldly-wise managerial skills and support mechanisms that companies half their size, in the more developed business world outside Indonesia, display in abundance. The costs of personnel, skilled, unskilled and managerial, are sharply rising due to improved educational and awareness levels, social programmes and global exposure, resulting in some reduction in industrial investments in the previously attractive countries of South East Asia. Singapore and Malaysia don't have enough people to meet their industrialisation targets, China, Indonesia and Thailand don't have enough graduates and engineers, China does not have enough Managerial and Marketing talent. Inexperience is rising to the top of corporations, emigration is reducing the pool of available skilled labour, poaching within countries and across country borders is endemic. Corporate responses range from paying whatever it takes to recruitment of first or even second generation Americans whose families originally emigrated from Korea or Taiwan and enticing them back to their roots, - and so the list goes on. But, Asia has huge numbers of people. How can the parts of the jigsaw be re-cut to fit better together and how many decades will this take to achieve?

There are one or two more encouraging pointers beginning to emerge. In themselves of relatively little consequence but if indicative of a trend, may be harbingers of better news for the future. Costs in Japan are reducing, both as far as wage increases are concerned and as a result of the creation of a larger pool of employees due to reduction in staffing requirements of the companies in recession, especially in the financial and computer services sector. Commercial rents in 1993 in Japan are down by as much as thirty-five per cent from the peak reached in 1989.

Due to the rapidity in growth of most enterprises in Asia, scant attention has been directed toward the future as the day-to-day internal growth issues have fully consumed management attention. Few companies in Asia, especially national ones, have sufficiently defined their philosophy, values, strategy, corporate culture and internal environment. They are not allocating enough time to determine in which markets or in which niches they intend to operate in today and beyond the year 2000. They are not taking time to define the resources, especially human, they will require and how to attract, develop and train these resources. All this in a backdrop where there is insufficient labour available today and on which forecasts show that this already poor situation will, during the next decade, further deteriorate. One of the more insidious affects upon companies of insufficient attention to planning and controlling the escalation in costs in Asia is that, while their sales turnover may be increasing at a very healthy rate, their profitability is relatively stagnant. Costs and lack of controls rapidly eat up the increases in gross margin. Until these enterprises take their future firmly in hand, their shareholder's dividend and thus the ongoing attractiveness of their companies to investors, will be poor.

The era of the rapidly growing Asian corporation expanding beyond its national boundaries began some years ago. Often, to local Asians, these companies are seen to be a preferred employer. This is because the intrinsic cultures are more readily understood and they usually offer more managerial authority and responsibility than does a Western company. This is very attractive to the hierarchically educated Asian national. Western multinationals are fast removing layers of management and, by empowering their employees, are forcing decision making much further down in the organisation. Although these companies would argue, often with much substance, that this makes for a more efficient and effective organisation, it inevitably has the consequence of either a perceived or actual reduction in scope of managerial authority. Many Asians today enjoy the power that comes with broad hierarchical managerial authority and, knowing they are more likely to achieve this in an Asian rather than Western multinational company, gravitate towards them. A marked trend can be displayed of competent Asian managers, having had years of experience and training with a Western multinational moving, at about the age of mid-thirties, to the large Asian national or multinational, even in situations where the compensation packages may be slightly inferior. These managers are moving for power and status reasons, their economic necessities of life having been adequately met.

The relevance to Asia of successful Western business models is fast reducing. The attitude of "what can they teach us anymore?" is rapidly developing in Asian management thinking. This arises from a number of factors, not least of which is the appalling recessionary situation in the West when compared to the sustained growth and profitability of Asian multinational and National companies. Moreover, educational standards amongst senior Asian business managers and governmental officials is fast improving. Put all this together with the inherent pride and relative insularity of Asian culture and one can readily begin to understand how the trend away from believing that "West is best" is developing considerable momentum.

There have been varied Western corporate responses to these problems such as pulling upon world-wide technology, training and employee development programmes, providing spells in the USA, Canada or Australia for employees to obtain second passports where this may be desirable and developing very imaginative regional and local compensation schemes. But they are all little more than band-aids on a gaping wound.

These problems force focus upon the recognition of Human Resources Management as a truly strategic tool for business improvement and that the real responsibility for the implementation of successful Human Resources policies lies with the line manager who has to correctly interpret the tone and guidance of those policies as set by the Chief Executive of the company. The Human Resources

Manager is there to provide the tools, techniques and quality checks but cannot be expected to be entirely responsible for improving morale, reducing turnover and providing developmental prospects for key employees. It is vital, however, that he or she be fully involved in all business strategy meetings and decisions, whether at board level or departmentally, so that the HR practices can be totally integrated to maximum effect within these strategies.

CHAPTER 2
USING HUMAN RESOURCES AS A
STRATEGIC TOOL OF MANAGEMENT

In the 1950's, industry was driven and managers were motivated by manufacturing activities. Products were designed to compliment the technological development of companies, plant capacity and capability. The 1960's dramatically increased awareness of the need for companies to be market driven rather than manufacturing driven and began the focus on what the customer requires rather than what could be made available to that customer. As industry became more focused and competitive, the 1970's saw the era of companies being tightly controlled from a financial point of view and many capable financial executives found themselves in the Managing Director's chair. In the 1980's emphasis shifted back again to consumers, but this time with the recognition that consumers exist both within and outside the company and so, Total Quality Management, Good Manufacturing Practices and Just In Time techniques began to be the means to achieve a competitive edge. It would seem that the 1990's is the era of striving for excellence in the management of Human Resources for, it can be reasonably argued that, because of good marketing, tight financial controls and excellent operating techniques having developed over the past four decades, almost all products have reached an acceptable quality standard and the only real definable difference between companies, the only real competitive edge remaining, is how they maximise and develop the motivation of their work-forces to provide that little extra added-value than do their competitors to the product or the service provided.

Today, it is essential for business success that the CEO recognises his role and responsibility in defining the Human Resources strategy of his company , enacts that strategy by example on a daily basis and encourages the Human Resources department to define and carry out policies consistent with that strategy. Perhaps we will not see too many Human Resources Managers reaching the absolute top in the organisation, but that top spot must be occupied by a person who has either had direct experience in the Human Resources function or is well-versed in its techniques and activities.

The trend in business schools today would also seem to support the recognition of the importance of the CEO taking the lead in defining the Human Resources strategy for their company and there are many case studies, both successful and otherwise that are being utilised to get the point across.

The awakening in Asia of the importance of the Human Resources role is reflected in the number of senior appointments now being made in the function, especially in countries such as Korea, Japan and Indonesia where hitherto little importance was attached to the professionalisation of this role which was historically seen as little more than a welfare function. Human Resources specialists are amongst the top three professional functions now being sought by executive placement companies throughout the Asian region.

Despite the necessity for competitive success in Asia, it would appear that companies more reluctantly than willingly, are being forced to place less emphasis on gain and greed and more concern on people, quality, customers and the environment. Employees are asking for and being treated more as individuals although somewhat paradoxically, there is also much emphasis being placed on the development of teamwork within enterprises. Increasing internationalisation of companies and shorter product life cycles are, in themselves, encouraging more rapid strides in technical innovation and subsequent people motivation. As customers become more educated and therefore more knowledgeable they demand higher standards of service and quality which can only emanate from a well-motivated work-force who recognise that the company is putting them first.

Organisationally, the hierarchy of management is becoming much flatter and more decentralised with increased responsibility for the developing globalisational aspects of business, creating a situation which begins to force greater employee involvement in business understanding and development, objective setting and understanding and contributing to corporate goals and strategic plans. This all augurs well for companies who recognise and embody these directions within their strategic Human Resources developmental programmes and forces rapid adaptation to new trends and organisational changes. It means change too in the Human Resources function which must be seen to have a key strategic role in the management and direction of the company. In order to be able to fulfil this role authoritatively, it is necessary that the leader of the Human Resources function displays a complete understanding of business and that he or she is not branded simply as an HR specialist rather than as the business person that is required. This means the function must be integrated at all levels into the strategic development of the business. It must be seen in the boardroom as well as in the departmental Sales, Production and other functional areas. The Human Resources function must take the lead in moving from the heavy tools of management to easy-to-use tools. From four pages of position description to one, from laborious performance management and appraisal systems to simple and effective ones, from a myriad of forms and files to a few floppy discs, from rigidity in compensation practices to reasonable, business driven, flexible structuring.

Creating a competitive advantage with Human Resources strategies means, in brief, to motivate employees to add greater value than your competitor. What are some of the techniques which can be employed and how can one measure the success of individual techniques? Measurement by sales or profit per head or by employee attitude surveys have all been used to good effect by many companies but perhaps a more intriguing measurement is that of the vitality ratio of employees. This essentially monitors their contribution by comparing added-value per capita to cost per capita. When this measurement is then benchmarked against competitors, the vitality ratio of your company becomes a meaningful measurement of employee efficiency and motivation. A low vitality ratio will mean low added-value and a resulting poorer service to customers which will, in turn, be reflected in lost sales and reducing revenue. The Canadian Manufacturing Association in a survey of a year or so ago, found that out of every one hundred customers, sixty-eight were lost because the employees of the company were indifferent and showed lack of interest in the company. A high vitality ratio means your competitive position is strong. It also assists in creating a realism in positioning salaries and benefits. There is little point in being in the third or upper quartile in compensation practices if your vitality ratio is lower than that of your competitors. One must be matched with the other.

Achieving enhanced employee vitality depends upon a consistent and well thought out strategic direction in Human Resources policies in the company. To what extent should teamwork be the style of behaviour, to what degree is it really appropriate to empower employees and involve them in helping to determine the strategic direction of the company? Teams are well proven in their effectiveness and are evolving into even greater areas of responsibility so that they are beginning to be refereed to as "super teams," - highly involved in decision making, scheduling and even employing, dismissing and determining salaries of other team members. Management has to provide the supporting environment, direction, information and tools to allow employees to be effective members of their teams and to creatively use their talents in the sharing of responsibility. An environment that allows employees to reach for the exceptional and not to fear repercussions in the event of mistakes should be a constant in every well managed company in Asia and, it is the job of the CEO, supported by the Human Resources specialist, to maintain that environment of trust and participation. This is sometimes difficult to do in some countries in Asia where the unfortunate business norm of not sharing knowledge with subordinates and not training them well because of a lack of feeling of personal security and confidence within the manager is an historical trait. Management must lead the way, encourage risk taking and innovation, providing an energetic, creative and caring environment in which people truly feel that they are making contributions which are valued, operated upon and that their individuality is respected and encouraged.

In a very thought provoking book published in 1992, Hal Rosenbluth of Rosenbluth Travel suggested that companies should put customers second and their own employees first. For only when people know what it is like to feel that they come first in someone's attention, will they themselves intrinsically be able to similarly put someone else first. This is a very translatable concept in any culture, including the cultures of Asia, but demands constant support from senior management and the embodiment of the idea in the core values and strategies of the company. In a similar vein, he suggests that companies recruit from non-conventional sources to provide new ideas and that a heavy emphasis be placed on recruiting 'nice' people on the basis that most other things can be taught. Niceness is however inherent in a personality. Nice people attract nice people who collectively do "nice", - i.e. the right things and care about others - i.e. the customer. Perhaps more businesses should consider, in their Human Resources policies, the strategic advantage of employing only nice people.

It is vital in the retention and development of human resources as a competitive edge in business to select employees as much for team fit as for individual contribution. Exceptional individuals are always going to be essential for certain growth areas of every company, but when those individuals become counter-productive to team effort and efficiency they often demotivate quite seriously other team members creating negative responses and a loss in efficiency far beyond acceptable levels.

Squelching bureaucracy is another way of improving employee vitality and increasing competitiveness. Removal of the protectionist memos or reports and the plethora of unnecessary documents and procedures, especially when that removal is suggested by the operatives themselves rather than by management can be highly motivating. Bench marking with other companies on the best of their procedures, whether they be in training, performance management systems, production techniques or social activities can be a rewarding mine of information leading to a consequent improvement in efficiency and morale. But nothing captures the imagination and moves employees to enhanced motivational effort more than honesty and openness in management. To open the financial books to employees, to train them in a fuller understanding of profit, loss, cash flow requirements and to keep them regularly informed of the position of the company engenders such a feeling of trust that it transcends the more petty problems of the day. To then supplement that knowledge with the display of a high ethical standard from the management of the company, enhances respect and loyalty. In a recent survey of 1,500 CEO's in twenty countries, ethics was rated as the most important personal characteristic for the global executive in the twenty-first century. Corporations must be above reproach because impeccable ethical standards will be indispensable to a firm's internal and external credibility. Human Resources programmes which have built high ethical standards are better able to inspire all employees to reach their potential. More and more HR departments are adding ethics training to their programmes. Hersey Foods and Pitney Bowes offer ethics awareness training for senior and middle level managers. GE has trained several hundred of its engineers in ethical reasoning and decision making. Ethics is what converts the values of the organisation into action, they establish the boundaries.

Open partnerships with customers and suppliers based on trust and mutual support further encourages a sense of belonging within the workforce and a greater feeling of purpose in their everyday life. If the operators know specifically from where the part came that they are fitting to another and then specifically to where it goes and what it does engenders greater pride, enthusiasm and care in their work.

One of the major doors which should remain constantly open if a company is to use its human resources to create a competitive edge is the training door. It must never be closed, whether in good economic times for the company or in poor, for the learning status of the workforce and their knowledge, when superior to that of their competitors, is what places their company ahead and keeps it there. The day when the competitor's learning status is the same as your own, is the day you have lost your competitive edge. Training should be perpetual, available to all and constantly reaching for new horizons. The trainers should be highly respected professionals, successful in their own discipline and on secondment for a year or so at a time to the training function to help maintain its life and vitality. The Training Manager should be a senior person in the organisation with direct access to the CEO who should set the strategic direction for training just as he does for overall Human Resources.

Companies who do not "give up" on their plateaued employees but continue to train them for lateral moves of differing responsibilities are the winners for often such plateaued employees cannot be easily removed from the company anyway and consume expenses and occupy chairs which halt the growth of others. If their energies and knowledge, which can be considerable, can be redirected by sensitive training and placement, then everyone benefits.

Some organisations have very aggressive targets for training, and rightly so. Corning Glass expects all employees to spend five percent of their time at work on training, this translates to ninety-two hours or two and a half workweeks per employee per year. Motorola calculates that for every $1 it spends on training, it has a return of $30 in productivity gains within three years. Yet, this is occurring in a context where just 15,000 employers, - a mere 0.5% of the total - account for 90% of the $30 billion spent on training annually in the USA (American Society for Training and Development). Clearly there is a long way to go, even in the United States, which boasts a ratio of trainers to workers of 1:122 whereas in most Asian countries the ratio is at best, 1:1000. (Germany has 1:49).

In summarising, we may conclude that there are certain strategies to be employed in the management of human resources to ensure that your company has the best competitive edge possible. They include ensuring that the CEO sets the mission, strategy and style of Human Resources policies in the company and then takes full ownership of them. In addition, it is now becoming essential that your Human Resources specialist is a fully rounded businessman who realises that happiness in the workplace is a strategic advantage and that the ability to learn faster than competitors is essential to retaining the lead; this all in a context of employees being allowed extensive creativity. For people support much more strongly something which they themselves helped to create than something which is imposed upon them.

It is well to reflect on and to remember one of the more erudite statements from Jack Welch, CEO of General Electric. "The distilled essence of competitiveness is that reservoir of talent and creativity and energy that can be found in each of our people. That essence is liberated when we make people believe that what they think and do is important - and then get out of their way while they do it."

CHAPTER 3
TRENDS IN COSTS AND SUPPLY
OF EXECUTIVES IN ASIA

Generally, at the lower and middle-management level positions, salaries throughout Asia are significantly below those paid for similar positions in Europe, Japan and the USA. Germany holds the place as the highest payer in the world, recruiting its executives at around US$50,000 per annum. It is closely followed by Tokyo, then, at a little distance, the west coast of the USA and London. In Asia the highest payer on recruitment is Sydney and the lowest, excluding China, India and Indo-China, is Manila where the recruitment salary for executives is well below US$10,000 per annum. Singapore, Hong Kong and Taipei fall quite centrally at about US$20,000 per annum.

At the senior and top management level, although the top three payers remain Germany, Tokyo and the west coast of the USA, Singapore jumps ahead of the rest of Europe, including London and also becomes the highest paymaster in Asia (other than Japan). It is closely followed by Hong Kong and Taipei whereas Sydney begins to drop precipitously until, at top management level in Asia, it is ahead only of Manila and seriously behind Seoul, Bangkok and Jakarta.

The differential in salaries between top and entry level managers is a fascinating comparison showing that whereas in Sydney or Frankfurt this differential is only about 2.5 or 3 times, in Jakarta and Bangkok it is as much as 11 times and even in Singapore it is about 7 times. Should this differential continue and there is every sign that it will because of lack of supply of senior managers throughout most of Asia, we can expect to see growing unrest and dissatisfaction from the educated middle-management level and real social discontent in the lower levels of companies and in society.   Human Resources Managers in Asia must prepare their plans to counter such problems, the least of which may be further unionisation amongst skilled and unskilled workers.

Often companies talk about the considerable increases they are forced to give to their management staff in Asia and complain about lack of supply which forces salaries to these high levels, however, there is another factor to be considered, inflation. The comparison of inflation with salary increases offers information on what the real benefit of the increase is to that manager and this comparison is more truly indicative of where the problem of supply really lies. In Tokyo, for example, increases are running at around 2.5% whilst inflation is at 2%, the manager thereby receiving a real benefit of only about 0.5%. This is to be contrasted with Jakarta where salary increases are of the order of 15% in a situation where inflation is about 6% or in Bangkok where increases are around 11% and inflation in the region of 5%. The benefit in terms of a real increase for managers in Hong Kong or Sydney, after discounting inflation, is around 1.5% but rises to between 4% to 9% in all the other major capitals of Asia being directly related to supply.

One of the consequences of this is that although managerial salaries are rising disproportionately to both inflation and lower level income, South East Asia still retains an overall cost advantage especially for the manufacturing industry, but in a developing climate of social inequality probably leading to increased unrest. Hourly wages in Malaysia, The Philippines and Thailand are between US$0.50 cents to US$1 whereas in Indonesia this drops to about 25 cents. This, in comparison to Singapore, Korea and Taiwan where the wages are approximately US$4 per hour. North East Asia would now appear to be in fairly close parity with Europe and the USA as far as costs are concerned but has the advantage over them of continuing higher economic growth ensuring sustained demand. A most interesting area for the corporate Human Resources Manager to now consider is that, because salaries of senior and top managers in Asia are on a par with or closely approaching those of both the USA and Europe, international pay scales become possible where top managers, wherever they are located in the world, are paid the same basic salary, their differentiation being related only to performance bonus or, exceptionally, to some expatriate benefits.

During the next decade, the supply of new executives to the workforce in Asia can first be indicated by an inter-country comparison of the educational profile of the workforce. It is interesting to note that whereas 46% of the total country's workforce in the USA are either in university or post secondary education, in Singapore, perhaps somewhat surprisingly, the figure is only 22%. However, this compares favourably to Malaysia at only 5% and to Indonesia which, with more than seventy-eight million workers, has only 20% of the work-force with more than an elementary school education and, desperately, only 1% with a university education. There are more positive signs elsewhere in the region where South Korea can boast a perhaps surprising 50% of its work-force in university or post-secondary studies which is considerably higher than Hong Kong, at only 40%, the same as Taiwan but still less than its aggressive neighbour Japan, at 80%.

The absolute number of students currently studying in Asian universities gives us a further indication of the availability of managers for the future although these numbers have to be treated with some caution because of differing university standards. It is likely that an applicant for a particular position in Singapore may only have to possess reasonable "A" levels to secure the position whereas in Manila the same position would call for a degree from a recognised Philippino university. Be that as it may, the picture of university students throughout Asia is worth studying.

At one extreme we may count well over two million students in universities in each of the countries of China, India and Japan whereas in Hong Kong, Malaysia and Singapore the figures hover around 50,000 for each country. In Australia we can see about 500,000 students (its smaller neighbour of New Zealand having only 150,000). In Taiwan the number grows to about half a million whereas in Thailand, South Korea and The Philippines the number well exceeds one million. Even this is not a complete picture as we should also consider the trend of Asian students studying in Western Universities which continues to grow unabated and also provides further indications for the future availability of managers. From the mid 1980's to the beginning of the 1990's we have seen a 74% growth in students from Hong Kong studying in Western universities. From Singapore, South Korea and mainland China the increase has been around 50% whereas from India it has been 94% and from Japan 132%. It is interesting to note that the mainland Chinese are both the highest in absolute numbers and the fastest growing group. The average growth rate over the past few years of all Asian students has been around 15%. In the USA, 60% of foreign students are from Asia and of these, 75% are registered in practical career oriented courses such as commerce. The remarkable number of 250,000 students return each year to Asia from Western universities but this is unfortunately a somewhat insignificant number when compared to the requirement of Asia and is also somewhat out of balance in terms of location of those requirements. For example, in Hong Kong there would now appear to be developing somewhat of a glut of returnees both from universities and from the disillusionment of Canada and the USA which, although providing the sought after second passport is, in these recessionary times, offering little opportunity for career advancement. Many companies in Hong Kong are wary of hiring returnees for if they are not correctly placed in an organisation, they can create a high degree of alienation amongst existing staff. The extra skills such returnees have gained in their studies and work overseas is certainly of value but do not, in the competitive situation of Hong Kong, necessarily translate into significantly higher salaries or benefits and due consideration is frequently taken of the loyalty of employees who have remained with the company in Hong Kong rather than seeking betterment abroad. A suspicion in employer's minds exists in recognising that many returnees have come back because of the availability of better jobs and higher salaries in Hong Kong than in Europe or the USA and not out of any feelings of loyalty to either their old company or to the colony itself. In addition, many employers wonder whether the returnees are likely, with their new passports, to be on the move again around the critical date of 1997.

The many factors impacting the supply of executives vary quite dramatically from one Asian country to another. The availability and standard of education is, of course, a fundamental one as is government policy in terms of percentage of budget or GNP allocated to educational support. Trends in migration considerably affect supply and we are currently seeing much movement from India to parts of South East Asia of executives especially in the field of Information Technology. Although demand for labour in China is growing, the country still has a very large supply of excess workers. Interestingly, the same cannot be said any longer for The Philippines where demand is growing faster than supply and that, although in 1993 it will still have about 100,000 excess workers, it cannot be reliably depended upon to be the provider of labour to other Asian countries for very much longer.

In South Korea, Singapore and Taiwan, according to various demographic studies from the late 1980's, the growth of the labour force is expected to virtually halve in the latter part of the 1990's. Japan will also have a continuing labour deficit and will see an absolute reduction in the size of its workforce because of its rapidly ageing population and reduction of entrants into that work-force thereby creating the requirement for far greater numbers of immigrant workers. One of the major flows of human capital in Asia over the next decade and beyond will be that from China to Japan. China being an obvious choice because it is close to Japan and has cultural, albeit colonial, ties and people who can master the oral and written forms of Japanese better than most foreigners. However, Japan like other countries of Asia, will have to modify their health, educational services and workmen's compensation practices to be more accommodating to the migrant workers they need or will find themselves with considerable problems of social conflict from these continually disadvantaged workers.

The expanding economies of Asia demand high quality executives not least of which should be found in Government positions. However, some countries, unlike Singapore, are not so advantaged as to be able to attract and retain the required executives. In Singapore often the managerial positions in government command high salaries and lead those in the private sector thereby attracting the best talent available. A few short miles away, across the causeway into Malaysia, the reverse is true, whereby the government, which wishes to considerably reduce its visible cost, does so by keeping salaries and benefits for government employees fairly low. A balance must be found in the countries of Asia as to who "leads" and who "lags" for without it, government encouragement for industrial development, disseminated through its officials, can be both out of balance and inappropriate. Indonesia, which has a tremendous dearth of quality management in comparison with its rapid pace of development deals with the problem of the shortage of managers by "importing" executives. Nearby Malaysia and The Philippines are the most popular hunting grounds. Some firms even go as far afield as Australia, Europe and the USA. Often expatriates are hired for three to five years in order to train the local middle managers.

A willingness to be expatriated also has a most meaningful effect upon the availability of executives. They are, of course, in a very different category from that of the migrant worker who usually moves on a relatively short-term basis to the affluent neighbouring countries. The Asian executive expatriate is a most necessary "evil" for the developing economies especially of South East Asia but the brightest and best often have severe problems in accepting such expatriation.

The most extreme case is probably that of the average Singaporean executive who cannot see any advantage whatsoever in leaving his or her well-ordered environment in which there is excellent education for children, a situation of splendid cleanliness and safety and an infrastructure of health care and governmental support second to none in Asia. What can motivate such an executive and his family to reside in the "grim pollution" of Bangkok, the "danger" of Jakarta or Manila or the "unfriendliness" of Hong Kong. Besides, their concern for reintegration into their companies at a more senior position on their return to Singapore is a very real one in an environment where insularity and unbridled local success continues unabated. In China it is estimated that some ten million managers need training before they can become sufficiently effective to contribute to the economic goals of that country and it is interesting to note that some firms there are now spending considerable amounts of money on in-house training and local management schools, especially in the hotel sector where a shortage of skilled workers has hit the industry extremely hard. In many Asian companies, inexperience is rising to the top because of the lack of the necessary expertise. This is especially evident in Indonesia and Thailand but is prevalent throughout Asia. Some corporate responses have included the recruitment of more rather than fewer expatriates, paying whatever it takes to attract and retain managers and recruiting from ex-nationals in North America for positions in Korea and Taiwan. The longer term perspective for Human Resources Managers in Asia requires the development of plans which create opportunities because of company reorganisation, most probably linked with dissemination of headquarters control and position to local autonomous units, enlarging the managerial pool by cross border transfers and developing highly professional in-company training facilities which may go as far as the creation of a company university or similar. Sheraton Hotels Asia Pacific has, for example, joined with the Bond University of Australia to provide an MBA programme for its executives. It expects that over the next five years about two hundred and fifty of the company's managers will follow the programme thereby helping to ensure its future managerial talent pool for Asia. This promotion from within concept is generally cheaper than bringing in expensive executives and has a major positive impact on morale as the workforce do not see all the "plum" jobs going, time after time, to outsiders.

Thailand has been somewhat slow to see the value of in-house training centres but is now moving substantially forward in creating such structures especially in the hospitality and retail industries. An interesting phenonomen is occurring in Japan where Japanese companies, against all tradition, are beginning to hire executives from the outside. This used to be unacceptable in Japan because of the concept of company lifetime employment and loyalty standards and the strong feeling that it was bad for morale as well as creating unfavourable relations between companies. However, times are changing in Japan, promotion by seniority is not now exclusively the norm, the trend towards merit promotion and pay and increased job mobility is developing and younger employees are placing less emphasis on their jobs and more on their personal lives thereby seeking employers who demand fewer hours and the freedom to take vacations without feelings of guilt.

A rather insidious movement in certain countries of Asia relates to the provision of "golden handcuffs" to selected management personnel who are remaining in the "custody" of the employer because of a very attractive compensation package related to years of service. This can often take the form of a Provident Fund Scheme which after usually ten years of employment can give a most attractive financial benefit to the employee. Prior to that tenth year, however, the vesting of the scheme often remains quite paltry. It is anathema to try to argue the morality of such schemes especially when faced with the realities of the lack of availability of good managers throughout Asia today, however, one cannot help but wonder what the ultimate real cost of such schemes will be, and not just in financial terms.

The senior manager of today in Asia has to possess a full and almost impossible to find, collection of skills. He or she must have excellent people management skills and leadership ability, sound financial business understanding, a multi discipline business knowledge, excellent public relations ability, in-depth knowledge of the culture of the country, the company, and the workings of headquarters. In addition a good conception of long-term planning and short-term focus are useful attributes as is absolute fluency in the language of the headquarters of the company, of the business language of Asia, English, and of the local language. An extreme sensitivity to the history and culture of Asia is called for, especially as it impacts the country of operation. All of this kaleidoscope he or she must

28

condense into a learning period often one half of that of his or her European or American counterpart for Asia cannot wait, its growth is too rapid and its requirement for local management skills and abilities is high today and ever growing.

CHAPTER 4
MANAGING PERFORMANCE IN ASIA

There is massive change occurring in Asia which is generated by high annual sales growth rates, often exceeding twenty per cent, alterations in manufacturing styles and distribution channels, a closer regional integration of markets and rapid increases in staffing and high turnover rates, especially of technically qualified personnel. Executive mobility throughout the region is rapidly developing and organisational structures are in a constant state of flux demanding much attention in recognising the need to successfully sustain flexible change management approaches. No company can afford to accept low levels of efficiency and must ensure that costs are tightly controlled. Added-value from all areas of the company, especially its employees, must be maximised and this demands the establishment and development of appropriate performance management systems.

There have been many "traditional" arguments in Asia concerning the inappropriateness of imposing performance management systems. Culturally, it is argued, they are unacceptable. It is unnatural to criticise colleagues in an open fashion. Performance is based more on personal relationships than on anything else. Most large companies have successfully grown without the benefit of such schemes, so the perceived need for them is low. Team-work, inherent in the Asian work ethic, suffers from the individualism of performance management schemes which have criteria difficult to objectively measure. The focus of such schemes is too narrow and does not allow for entrepreneurship and, anyway, pay rises are pretty good throughout Asia so performance management schemes are unlikely to provide the average employee with greater incentive or reward than he or she currently enjoys.

Many of these arguments have more than a grain of truth to support them but fundamentally, the business world is too small and competitive to allow a "laisser-faire" non measurement attitude especially amongst technical and managerial staff. The key is to adapt or create the performance management system to local country and company culture. What works in New York will not work in Tokyo. So, it is necessary to design one system for New York operations and a different one for Tokyo and, because there is the need to provide

30

quality and validity throughout the organisation, ensure an end-point which can be commonly accepted and measured so that fair comparisons can be made between all locations in the group. After all, if this can be achieved at the job or position evaluation stage for grading and remuneration purposes, - it should also be possible at the performance management level.

As well as cultural considerations, there are a few fundamentals that should be embodied in any performance management system. These include ensuring an open, honest and non-threatening environment for review sessions. Realistic objectives must be set and reviewed periodically rather than simply left for an annual appraisal. Performance management is not performance appraisal. Performance should be constantly managed, not simply appraised after the fact. High performance should be reinforced through praise, recognition and, perhaps increased responsibility, whereas low performance requires encouragement through coaching and counselling. There must be clarity in the objectives and allowance for external influences affecting the achievement of objectives should be made. The individual's objectives should be integrated with those of his supervisor and relate to the overall mission and objectives of his or her unit and to those of the company. Negative feedback should be removed and the focus of the review sessions must be on results rather than on behaviour.

When you consider it, evaluation of performance is an inevitable part of life. We perform it at home with our family and friends, it is performed at school with our children - who always see the results. Even those companies who boast they have no need of such a system generally evaluate performance at annual salary or merit review time. Some companies in Asia, unfortunately quite a number, have a written format for employee performance assessment which often is not seen or even shared with employees - unlike school, college or university! Suddenly we are being appraised, our livelihoods and futures being affected and we are not told about it. Even when performance review or appraisal interviews are reported as occurring in a company, they can often be either demotivating judgmental sessions or superficial ten minute affairs. When they are, often the reason is that the interviewer is uncomfortable with the process, unsure of himself or herself because of lack of interview technique and cultural awareness and wants to get the unpleasant task over with as quickly as possible. So, managers often pretend they do not need to do the interview as they already know very well everything that is happening in their department and are sufficiently close to their subordinate not to have the need for a formal review. It has to be said that subordinates too have ambivalent feelings towards performance appraisals. They are happy to receive feedback on how they are performing, - but only when that feedback is favourable. No-one wants to hear that their performance is perceived as being below standard or they themselves are not as highly regarded as they had believed.

In most performance management systems it is implied that what is achieved is what is important, i.e. results oriented, and that those results can be objectively measured. Although largely true, we have to remember that in Asia, we can face many problems by using this approach. For example, in Japan, there is more concern with judging a person's integrity, morality, loyalty and co-operative spirit than on achieving high sales volume. Furthermore, for the Japanese, the notion of "objective" truth is usually neither important or useful. "Objectivity" refers to the foreigner's point of view while "subjectivity" refers to the host's viewpoint.

Giving direct feedback at review or appraisal sessions must take into account "saving face" so crucial to Asian cultures. Confronting an employee with failure in an open direct manner would be considered tactless and barbaric. Appraisal also assumes that the feedback given will be used to correct or improve upon past performance. This requires that individuals receiving the feedback are willing to evaluate themselves instead of blaming others or external conditions for their performance. This assumes that man has control over the environment and is able to alter the course of events, a viewpoint alien to Confucian teaching. It also assumes that what will happen in the future is of importance and that the past can be used as a guide to future behaviour. Again, concepts alien to much of the thinking embodied in the education of Asians.

When creating or developing a performance management system, it is well for us to remember that the company's perception of the role and success factors it attaches to a particular position or individual may vary substantially from those of the individual's own perception. It is therefore imperative that a "performance contract" of some nature be agreed between the two parties. This contract has no legal validity, it is simply a realistic clarification of agreed upon goals having a totally objective measurement of results. It should, correctly used, promote an atmosphere of mutual understanding, confidence and objectivity between both parties and give the position holder a clear understanding of what is expected of him or her. But, especially in the Asian environment, it should not be over used or become the be-all and end-all of the performance management system, for to do so may cause the very downfall of that system. Participants may consider that it is too rigid and dogmatic. Minimisation of forms, procedures and paperwork should be an overall objective when creating or amending a performance management system.

Conflict in the review and appraisal interview situation must be minimised. The interviewer's conflicting roles of coach and judge require competent sensitivity as does the handling of the interviewee whose need for praise must be tempered with objective assessment. Uncomplicated paperwork which should not be seen to be akin to any form of checklist, will help to develop a reasonably structured but also free-ranging discussion. A non-territorial environment for the interview itself, such as a comfortable side area of a conference room or the quiet corner of a hotel room will more readily put both participants at their ease.

A problem solving and two way communication interview, having aspects of mutual or even upward appraisal, is a very healthy environment to promote in performance management techniques. However, in Asia, such an approach is not readily understood and is difficult to manage as respect for authority is so deeply ingrained that questioning or disagreeing with one's superior is generally an unacceptable behavioural trait. Such attitudes may be changing but very gradually, so, when designing a performance management system and giving interview technique training in Asia it must always be done with a full understanding that culture is of paramount importance.

Attitudes to avoid during the interview process include superficiality whereby the reviewer does not prepare sufficiently well enough for the interview or feels so uncomfortable in the interview situation his statements and advice are bland, unprovocative and do not assist in developing improvement ideas. To be too directive in the interview is also likely to provoke a negative response from recipients, especially in Asia where there are many aspects to be taken into account when considering performance and where ambiguity may be a valuable tool in developing positive performance improvements.

The effectiveness of the review interview can be gauged to some extent by whether the supervisor really tried to understand the subordinate and if the supervisor's feedback was clear and specific leading to a culmination of unforced mutual agreement and understanding. External influences affecting performance should also be covered and it would be an added bonus if the reviewer purposely strove to learn more about the true feelings and values of the person being reviewed. Overall, however, it must be accepted that the quality of the performance review and the successful application of a performance management system is largely dependant upon the nature of the day to day relationship between the parties to that review and system.

34

CHAPTER 5
MANAGING CROSS CULTURALLY

Much has been written and experienced concerning aspects relating to cross cultural management. There is a lot of hype about the subject but, increasingly and thankfully, there appears to be a greater realism developing, concerning the similarities of management success irrespective of culture together with the utilisation of simple but effective ways of coping with the challenge and pleasure of cultural differences.

Hopefully, the days of companies relinquishing their corporate and operational culture in favour of complying with local culture, - wherever that culture resides, - are disappearing. We are all aware of the horror stories of Asia, particularly in the developed and smaller "dragon" countries of North East Asia where, because of our acceptance of lack of knowledge of local culture we appoint, as CEO and as our senior management, nationals of that country, only to find out five years later that our company is no longer our own, its values not ours, its control and culture independent of head office, leaving us little recourse but to sell our equity back to our "partners" whose partnership objectives we now understand to be diametrically opposed to our own.

The message we should all have learnt by now is, assuming you have a corporate culture of which you are justly proud, protect it, do not relinquish it. Capture and explain it to the new host country. Live the culture within your new company. Be proud of it, never apologetic, sell it constantly. If small adaptations are necessary because of real lack of understanding or language interpretation or communication problems, adapt slightly but not much - and don't give up. Your ethical standards, your operating principles should be good for any country in the world in which you operate. If they aren't, then change them on a world-wide basis not simply locally.

One thing all businessmen understand, the world over, is results and that good performance should in some way be better rewarded than poor performance. Some cultures, some governments may not easily allow this reward situation to take effect, but that does not mean that it is not understood. The myth surrounding a company's inability to reward superior performance by an individual or a team in, for example, Korea or Japan, is just that - a myth. The problem is simply how to recognise that performance without others losing "face" or the superior performer being given too much face. A manager capable of feeling the pulse of his organisation - and every manager's aim must be to do just this - will know how best to create a suitable reward structure. A night out on the town in Tokyo with the sales team making fun of the 'luck' of a great breakthrough by a colleague may be far more appropriate than a solemn ceremony awarding him a monetary or symbolic gift. Manage your company by results wherever you are located but ensure you reward in a way appropriate to the culture, both company and country, in which you operate.

People's understanding of the value of a team approach being superior to an individual approach to get something done, or even to make the decision on what has to be done, is universally recognised. Many cultures, especially in Asia, are team-centred cultures where group consensus is vital. Even in the individualistic USA, recognition of the value of team working is high. The internal workings of a team may differ by culture but, fundamentally, if you create a team and are naturally able yourself to be a valued team member, then such an approach transcends cultural difficulties.

Business practices vary by country, by culture. What might be regarded as being illegal or at least highly questionable in one cultural situation is most definitely acceptable in another. However, ethical standards of operation for companies venturing abroad should not be compromised. Training in desired ethical behaviour which complies with the company's culture should be given to all managers whether they journey beyond their shores or stay at home. They set the standards for their organisations. Professional businessmen would rarely argue that corrupt or doubtful practices are essential to the successful development of their businesses. They understand what is acceptable or not and why their companies and themselves must comply with reasonable ethical standards. Reasonability tests may sometimes have to be devised or instructed by the headquarters of a company, but some elements are immutable such as the obvious unacceptability of bribes or favours to government officials, even if "the other guy is always doing it". Reasonable standards are often dictated by law makers and pockets of progress are being made today in Asia, even in Korea and Thailand, but it is the responsibility of every company to define what it means by reasonable ethical standards of behaviour for its employees and agents and to ensure it communicates and sustains them throughout its organisation.

Leadership by managers transcends culture. The expectation everywhere, in every culture, is that the manager should lead. Whether he or she leads autocratically or as a coach is somewhat dependent upon personal style but should also be highly dependent upon the local culture. Leadership styles which succeed well in Boston may fail miserably in Japan, but the true leader should have that within him or her which, maybe after some false starts, allows sufficient flexibility in outlook and style to adapt to local circumstance. Leadership is, after all, getting the best results from your people with their co-operation and a study of local attitudes and characteristics by leaders prior to attempting their leadership role, is mandatory. The style of leadership practised by President Dwight D. Eisenhower, when he was a general leading the allied forces in Europe in World War Two holds good for most cultures. He illustrated his concept of leadership by the simple example of having a piece of string on his desk and reminding his colleagues, "pull it and it will follow you wherever you want to go, push it and it will go nowhere." Effective leadership transcending culture also demands that the leader never asks a subordinate to do something he is not prepared to do himself. No matter how menial the task, if, from time to time, the leader is seen to bend his body to the task along with his colleagues whilst still being able to retain the necessary presence, he will have closed a gap which cultures have forced apart.

It is important for us to reflect that people generally work for people not for a company. This is particularly true in many countries in Asia, perhaps most notably, in Thailand where the two most important cultural influences are that life comes before work and the boss before the company. Because of education, culture and tradition, Thai's naturally lack experience in the field of decision making in business and may often prefer autocratic management. Although this is expected to gradually change over time, wise business leaders in Thailand should temper their modernistic management ambitions with realistic understanding of what their colleagues are looking to them to deliver.

Cultural training and language awareness does much to assist in the removal of cross cultural difficulties but too many companies are blinkered in their training approaches in that they train only the manager new to the location and not the spouse and children who are equally affected and major contributors to the success or failure of the expatriation. The benefit of the "recipients" of the expatriate also undergoing cross cultural training is becoming more recognised. Take for example, the situation of the establishment of a manufacturing operation in a rural province of mainland China. Heading up the operation is a Swede, his engineers are American and his operational supervisors are Hong Kong Chinese. Can you imagine the enormous cultural difficulties for the Chinese operators, hitherto knowing only traditional methods of working which have never involved performance measures, profit and loss considerations, market place requirements and so on. The company looking for a successful entry into a cultural environment new to them should prepare their "accepting" employees to understand what is being imposed upon them!

Many Asians in the working environment consider that sharing their knowledge and experience is a kind of favour, not necessarily part of their duty. Cross cultural training should carefully inject development sharing roles, their benefits and the need to build excellent interpersonal relationships and trust to facilitate the sharing of knowledge. Expected managerial efficiency improvements must be tempered with reality as often Asian employees will not support the promotion of a person with higher education over a person who is older, worked in the company longer and has more experience. Promoting a less competent manager of the right age and experience may result in a more efficient workforce than would come from the promotion of an apparently excellently qualified younger person.

Bridging cultural gaps is sincerely aided by consistency in bringing the two "camps" together in small social gatherings. In some Asian countries, for example The Philippines or Thailand, these gatherings may include families, in others such as Korea or Japan, probably will not. The purpose of the gathering is to allow more intimate cultural understanding and sharing by redefining and understanding mutual goals divided by cultural norms. Happy hours and pre-meeting socialising work well in all countries in Asia.

Perhaps the most telling of all activities which ensure rapid cross cultural acceptance is if the person appointed to a new cultural environment can really display a true interest and inquisitiveness in trying to come to grips with the host country's language and culture.

It would be unreasonable to expect rapid fluency in either, but those managers who truly make an effort to understand and, however faultingly, stammer a few words of the language of the host country, go a very long way to becoming personally accepted. If, especially in Asia, they can tie these attributes to that of an appreciation of the cultural norm of ambiguity rather than clarity in conversation and decision making and the overwhelming goals of consensus and compromise rather than conflict, their acceptance will become more complete. People who adapt well cross culturally, are usually secure within themselves, have a strong sense of humour and fun and are calmly confident of their beliefs and values in life. This emotional stability and strength benefits well from being challenged by new cultural norms and ideas. The less emotionally stable person has a much more difficult time in adapting to and accepting different norms than his own. Ironically, the manager with an excellent track record at home is often the worst choice for a cross cultural position. Those who excel in the fast moving marketing world of Europe or the USA are the most likely to fail in the laid back consensus, no conflict countries which make up most of the Asian continent. They will probably be seen to be rude, aggressive, and lacking in all sophistication. They will not engender respect.

Cross cultural management is an art. One requiring much patience and application and marked human relationship skills, but the rewards to the expatriate and his family of a successful sojourn in the host country are immeasurable and timeless.

CHAPTER 6
FACILITATING CHANGE IN ASIA

We have previously discussed the many conflicting pressures being brought to bear in Asia on the creation and enactment of strategic Human Resources policies. The need for highly-skilled businessmen who are simply not available in the required numbers, the movement to flatten layers of management whilst still attempting to meet the Asian manager's need for power and authority. The huge challenge of resurrecting business life in China in a backdrop of political uncertainty, are but a few of the problems to be solved.

So we must, if we are to survive in the fast-paced Asian environment, plan for and facilitate change in our companies, especially ensuring our ability to react quickly to the vitality and pressure for growth emanating from most Asian national organisations. How do we begin to facilitate this change? What are the building blocks? How long is the process? Perhaps the only one of these three questions to be easily answered is the third one for the process of change in Asia today is continuous, infinite. There is virtually no plateauing to be seen in business as there is throughout the USA and Europe. Change is constant, the need to facilitate and manage change is constant.

Change management training is in its infancy in Asia and the need for it is not perceived as particularly important especially in local and national companies. But many of these companies possess the technology and the market place availability to grow to a very considerable size, necessitating that they take cognisance of changes in organisational structure and behaviour to equip them to maximise their growth opportunities.

The requirement and support for change must be directed from the very top of the organisation. It is unlikely to successfully permeate from below. This necessitates that the CEO possess the wisdom and vision to recognise signals for change, - whether they be in the industrial or political environment surrounding the company or whether they emanate from the CEO's own longer-term strategies for the company. Recognising and then facilitating change is not something that is necessarily an inherent attribute of every CEO especially where his or her "in" box is already overflowing with problems of the day. It is therefore essential that either the CEO takes time out to understand and be trained in change management techniques or that the responsibility is delegated to a senior manager in the organisation. Delegation is acceptable, abrogation of responsibility for the CEO championing change, is not.

Some aspects of change may be fairly simple to enunciate. Clarity of vision and displaying continual support for it, is one, - empowering employees to make many of their own business decisions thereby moving towards a greater feeling of ownership which in turn encourages improvements in motivation and morale is another. So is the publication of a mission statement which employees can relate to rather than feel that it is little more than a collection of motherhood statements. A mission such as "We will consistently have a higher market share and profitability than company X" is directly measurable, definitive and immediate. People can relate to it and see to what extent progress is being made. Not only this, but every employee, when considering their own activities, have something very tangible to relate to. In effect, they are themselves able to use the mission of their company on a daily basis. Managers are key to implementing and sustaining change in the organisation. To be successful they must agree with vision and mission statements and even be an integral part of their creation, then they must be empowered to enact the vision and mission.

Environmental changes in Asia are occurring at a very fast pace forcing continual management alterations in direction, staff recruitment and management policies. For the management of the company to appear to be in control of the destiny of their company and thereby to be regarded as reliable employers, their only choice is to be seen to be managing the change process proactively rather than reacting to it after the event. To move from a policy of reduction in expatriates one year to having to reverse that policy and recruit more the following year because of market place constraints in availability of key management personnel is not consistent or controlled management.

To enter the market of Korea and then to exit three years later because "it's just too tough" shows a lack of preparation. To play with Indo-China in terms of "will we, won't we" invest, displays a lack of decisiveness which will be badly interpreted, especially by local staff who compare this type of management behaviour to that of the consistency and long term investment thinking of most of the

Asian races, especially the Japanese. Environmental considerations impacting change include economic, social, political, business and competitive activity. None can be ignored although some have greater impact than others depending upon the country in which the business is operating. Political considerations and awareness in The Philippines and India, are, for example, much more important to follow than is the placid stability of Singapore political life where you know today that next year will offer exactly the same situation for business as did last year.

The trend towards information based organisations is fast gathering momentum and offers alternative work habits for consideration by the enterprise. The manager's ability to work from his home based information power-house may necessitate less time in the appalling traffic of Bangkok or in the office itself. Conference calls, especially where video is used, alter the nature and necessity for international meetings. Regarding your company as an added-value rather than as a cost or profit enterprise has a major impact on changes in management style and behaviour. Total Quality Management priorities and the need to comply with ISO 9000 principles are beginning to dramatically effect Asian management behaviour and organisational structure as is environmental protectionism. One of the first questions being asked by a furniture wholesaler in the U.K. who is considering importing Korean chests is "Is the wood from environmentally protected forest stock or is it being plundered?" - until very recently, no-one in Korea even understood the question never mind having to justify an answer. Such world movements create dramatic change in business management in Asia.

Advances between multinationals of different countries and cultures to access one another's market places with complimentary products force an appreciation of change acceptance within the organisation and the awareness that although today the boss may be American, he can be Japanese next year and American again two years later. People have to be trained to accept how to live with such changes and be taught to realise the benefits and opportunities which can arise from them. If such change management is not regarded seriously and adequate preparation and training given, then the result will be employee frustration and confusion leading to reduced efficiency and competitiveness.

Rather, the company has to take account of all external influences

42

and attempt to gauge where it will be ten years from now. What type of organisation will it have, flat or hierarchical? How much will technology in its own business area as well as in the outside world, have advanced and how should the company utilise that advance? How volatile will the market have become and how sophisticated the customer? Flexibility in organisational structure and behaviour is ✓ called for. How will the organisation respond to this need for flexibility and what can be done now to prepare the way? Is our current company culture healthy or unhealthy and if we believe it cannot be sustained during the next decade what do we change, by when and how?

In the Asian business scene of today, every company has to enunciate what its strategic intent really is. Should it remain a niche player in its home market or should it broaden its product base and make a major investment, for example, in China? Is it clear about internationalisation, globalisation? Is performance management a core value of the company? Is social responsibility and environmental concern an integral part of corporate culture? Many huge Asian conglomerates have grown like "topsy" and now find themselves in many diverse market segments with confused knowledge of profitability or strategic direction by product group.

Many companies in Indonesia and Thailand find themselves operating in the business segments of tourism, construction, pharmaceuticals, oil, hotels, marinas and so on, with one board of management attempting to pull strategy and direction together for all these diverse areas and that board consisting of the second generation of the family probably with an average age of around thirty-two. A momentous task for the most sophisticated of boards, made even more difficult because of business inexperience and lack of sustained vision for the development of the company. It is now time to temporarily apply the brakes in these huge enterprises before they consume profit inappropriately and lead investors into economic distress.

✓ Once the company has been able to succinctly define its strategic direction it should then forecast its requirements over the next ten years. Determining what technological supports it requires, number and type of people and the skills they should possess, the proportion of employees taking managerial positions and what a managerial position will involve in their projected organisational structure for the next decade. Bearing in mind the availability of technical and managerial personnel in Asia and the expectations of this increasingly well educated and confident work force, this forecasting is critical for otherwise business growth targets become wish lists which will never meet reality. Once having forecast requirements and matched these against likely availability, it will probably become necessary to adjust target areas for growth either geographically or by product type and to re-think the organisational structure.

Having forecast requirements, an analysis of today's "inventory" needs to be taken. What are our core competencies? Have we a sufficiently detailed skills analysis of our existing people? Do our financial and accounting systems reflect the strategic direction of the business or are we still using methods of twenty or thirty years ago that are not measuring what we really need to have measured?

Do we only know contribution by product group at the gross margin level? Operating margin, which is reflecting total company activities, could be successfully hiding a product which has an excellent gross margin but costs so much to support that it becomes unprofitable at operating margin level. Can we identify it?

Do we have a good training needs analysis and assessment?

Are our employee and management development programmes and policies adequate to meet the ten year projected human resources requirements? Should we begin our own in-house MBA or diploma programme to develop and retain potential senior managers for the future?

These and many other questions must be answered by the change management team as they structure the business for the next decade. They should also investigate new trends in management and leadership, considering how they wish to alter the working style of the company to meet with employee's expectations.

In Asia, companies need their employees much more than the employees need their companies. The name of the game is how to attract, motivate and retain employees, for not being able to do so will result in restrictions in growth and profitability of the company. Enhanced employee job enrichment and involvement in the strategic direction and on-going management of the company is the obvious business solution during the next decade. How can hundreds of years of traditional family and hierarchical management style in Asia begin to accept this fundamental trend reversal? Those companies accepting it first, realising its inevitability and encouraging its employees to change, will be the ones at the forefront of the business scene in the twenty-first century in Asia.

CHAPTER 7
THE VITALITY RATIO

The conventional methods of managing effectiveness and efficiency of employees are most often related to comparing, on a year to year basis, sales per employee or perhaps profit per employee. This is achieved by the simple expedient of dividing net sales or net profit (usually net is preferred to gross) by the number of employees at the year's-end. It is a simple measurement but may not tell the full story of the activity or "vitality" of the company's workforce and, in not doing so, may result in precipitate and illogical actions being taken in for example, staff reduction, to meet what is perceived as reduced efficiency of employees. The truth of what is occuring in the business may lie elsewhere, shareholders may be taking too many dividends, sales programmes may be poor, product quality could be sub-standard, too much tax may be being paid. The list goes on.

A different way of contemplating the success of your business and the efficiency or vitality of your employees is to regard many of the traditional "costs" in your business as value-added activities and beneficiaries. Specifically, there are five components in your business - once you have bought your raw material, which add value to that raw material. They are :-

- **Shareholders**, who provide long-term funding which enables the business to develop and enact its strategic direction.
- **Banks**, and other short-term lenders who provide a ready supply of operating cash for today's needs.
- **The state**, providing the infrastructure of services by which means the operation of the company's premises and ancillary activities can function.
- **The company itself**, as it reinvests in more efficient plant and machinery.
- **Employees of the company**, who provide the labour and ideas creating the company's end product.

These five "components" are the added-value in the operations of every company. A wise company will track the contribution of these components, project them forward consistent with its longer-term planning horizon and then benchmark against competitive companies to determine where their own added-value may be insufficient or inefficient.

One major component of this benchmarking should be to use the data which has been created to determine the competitiveness of the company's vitality ratio with those companies with whom you are benchmarking. Vitality Ratio is calculated as follows ✓

- Determine the cost per capita by taking the added-value component as it relates to all employees and dividing by the number of employees.

- Determine the total added-value of the operation by adding together the five contributors, - personnel, company, lenders, government, shareholders.

- Determine the added-value per capita by dividing the total added-value by the number of employees.

- Divide the added-value per capita by the cost per capita - The result is The Vitality Ratio.

e.g.   **ADDED VALUE COMPONENTS**

	$'s
Employees	100
Shareholders	50
Loans	50
State	50
Company	50
TOTAL	300
Number of employees	50

Therefore : -

Cost per capita	= 100 divided by 50	= 2
Added value per capita	= 300 divided by 50	= 6
VITALITY RATIO	= 6 divided by 2	= 3

Having understood how to calculate Vitality Ratio, it can be used to determine what has been the historical trend of that ratio and to then intelligently forecast changes based upon either historical trend or agreed future business plans.

You are now able to set Vitality Ratio objectives for your company which directly measure the effectivity of your employees and cannot be clouded by business or cost issues extraneous to those relating to personnel, especially when personnel cannot have any influence, good or bad, upon the other elements.

This concept demands a change in thinking for many corporations who have to move from a position of regarding their employees as costs to believing them to be vital added-value contributors to the development of wealth within the organisation. Once this shift in thinking has occurred, it allows more appropriate consideration of how to nurture, retain and develop this essential wealth-creating contributor and leads to more realistic and equitable Human Resources strategies and policies.

48

CHAPTER 8
ATTITUDES TO EMPLOYMENT AND CAREERS

✓ The consideration of this issue falls into two camps, the "haves" and "have-nots." The haves being the better educated Asians enjoying the benefits of economic growth in countries such as Singapore, Hong Kong, Taiwan, Korea and, to a lesser extent Thailand. The "have-nots" is that generation in Asia facing little hope of improvement in their future because of the poor industrial infrastructure of their countries. These countries represent quite a mixture of stages of "have-not" but may be taken to be India, China, The Philippines, Indonesia and the entire Indo-China grouping of countries. Many of these countries are fast developing but, it is unlikely that any of them will compare, at least within the next decade, in educational, social, political stability and improved living standards with the more developed countries in Asia.

✓ Japan is likely to become the role model for developing economies in Asia and will have a major influence on Asian lifestyles. Its products are becoming increasingly visible throughout the whole of the region. The huge numbers of motor vehicles are now complimented with everything from televisions, videos and cameras to fast-food noodles and ginseng powder. The Japanese ability to produce high quality products and to package them attractively will become the standard throughout Asia.

✓ Singapore will act as the showplace of balance in Asia. Balance in politics, social awareness, opportunity, religion, the meeting of Eastern and Western cultures and will also assist further in developing an Asian individualism and arrogance which rejects the idea of any necessity of control or leadership by Western business establishments to the extent that the advantages of such liaisons may be pointlessly lost.

The eventual emergence of a real China superstate consisting of mainland China, Hong Kong and Taiwan, will create a major economic block not only within Asia and therefore opposing Japan, but also within the trading community world-wide. Indonesia, Malaysia, The Philippines and Thailand will continue to strongly develop but will lag somewhat behind the other major economies in the provision of educational support and social benefits. Consumers will demand enhanced personal care products, better health care home-care improvements, higher quality and even greater variety in food and more recreational and fitness facilities, the latter often expected to be provided by the companies for whom they work. Fashion, both for home and for the office will also see a continuous increase in quality and demand. During the next ten years in Asia there could easily be as many as four hundred million new consumers who will emerge from subsistence living to be within economic and physical reach of at least the basic consumer goods and services.

Companies defining their market advantage based on their core competencies and combining within their corporate cultures the traditional standards of friendship and the Confucian values of Asia with the best which Western educational tools and advances can supply, will steal a march on less well prepared competitors. The competitive advantage of these companies will be best displayed by the way in which they utilise their inherent human resources skills and how able they are to develop and retain these skills. It is a truism however that affluence and confidence breed arrogance and indifference quite different from the traditional life and work ethics hitherto seen in Asia. Hunger and the aggression necessary for success often emanates from poverty and deprivation. As the Asian countries become more affluent and as the workforce becomes more educated, an entire revolution in values and work habits will insidiously appear. It is already here today in one or two countries of Asia, perhaps most notably, Singapore. It is useful to take Singapore as a case study for it is likely that what is happening there today is but a precursor of what will eventually come to pass in the other fast developing major cities, especially of South-East Asia.

Singapore's rapid technological, social and economic advancement coming from a poor third-world country to the greatest port in the world, a major financial centre and a quality manufacturer of electronic items with an educated and intelligent work-force all in just twenty-five years is a phenonomen which now is in danger, if not carefully controlled, of consuming itself within its own trappings of success. It is the era of candidate power in Singapore. Too many successes breeding too many excellent middle and senior management jobs for too few locals. Tremendous emphasis is placed by the current Singaporean generation on wealth-creation. A typical conversation revolves around; "How much did you pay for...? How much more can you get for....? Which industry is now paying the highest salaries for...?" Relatively little discussion revolves around considerations of loyalty to employers and how to best assist their current company to grow.

These attitudes in the current work-force are further exacerbated by the declining population growth which has its roots in population policies of some thirty years ago. Even though the government of Singapore is trying to reverse the trend, it is now almost inbred within the Singaporean career woman of today that one, maybe two children at most is all that is "sensible."

The education system in Singapore has developed tremendously over the past two decades, but again at a cost. The learning by rote style to ensure full and standard quality education for all has created a dearth of entrepreneurs who wish to travel beyond Singapore's shores to create wealth and experience which can assist in further development of this attractive island state. It is remarkable to reflect on the aggressive growth and wealth creating activities of the same, equally well-educated, generation of Chinese nationals who are living and working in Malaysia, Hong Kong and Indonesia, in comparison with others residing in Singapore. The problem of high but standardised education and reasonably comfortable wealth stifling creativity and ambition is not a new one, but it is one to be studied and corrected whenever and wherever possible. Unfortunately, some of the more insidious types of working attitudes that are prevalent in Singapore are the "you owe me" attitude, "more pay, less work" attitude and "call me manager" attitude.

The "you owe me" attitude is apparent in the school and college leavers, but is especially noticeable in the students having completed their university education. Because of their superior intellectual standing, which, all their lives has been bolstered and encouraged by successive educational and political leaders, these new employees expect to receive immediate pay-offs in terms of money, recognition and promotion and, because of the shortage of such talent in Singaporean industry, they are in fact achieving their expectations, creating an even greater rod for industry's back in the future. Candidates are regularly choosing between employers according to how attractive they appear and the choice is made only for the time period whilst that attractiveness is retained.

"More pay, less work" is beginning to take a hold on much of the work-force of Singapore. With high salaries being achieved, Singaporeans are demanding the time to enjoy them. Asian norms and values where emphasis is placed on hard and continuous work are being rapidly eroded. The Singaporean generation of today wants 'quality time' on the golf-course, on vacations and by displaying examples of its wealth on the seas surrounding Singapore. Their companies, banks and government bodies continue to prosper phenomenally when compared with much of the rest of the industrialised world. Why should not the employees also share in the spoils to a greater extent than hitherto? Even employee's savings and housing opportunities are handled for them through the mechanism of the Central Provident Fund so, in essence, what they receive in their monthly take home pay, once basic living costs are removed, is all play money. And to play demands time.

The "call me manager" syndrome has its amusing side where advertisements for Sales Engineers have been replaced by the call for Marketing Executives and where no clerks exist any longer in Singapore as everyone is, at least, an executive assistant. Status is of huge importance in Singapore and, indeed throughout most countries of Asia. To be a technician, engineer or salesman is simply to have not yet arrived. At the lower levels of employment there are so very few Singaporeans willing to perform manual work that most construction workers and increasing numbers of nursing staff and employees in the social services are being imported from surrounding Asian countries, most notably Malaysia and Indonesia. This is beginning to create a strain upon the employment and immigration laws of Singapore as well as creating some political and environmental difficulties.

From a positive point of view it can be argued that most young Singaporeans "know what they want." They have ambitions for a certain life-style, earnings potential, family size and vacation programme. The clever employer is the one who analyses and accepts this inevitability and then builds within his human resources approaches, policies to meet these ambitions. He provides continuous education and employee development training programmes. He has sufficiently flexible grading and compensation programmes to continuously offer "promotional" opportunities. He offers real responsibility to untried youngsters. He provides children's crèches for the career mothers. He provides gym and work-out facilities for the fitness conscious employees as well as flexibility of working hours so that leisure opportunities can be in a controlled balance with the necessities of work. He offers incentives of visits abroad which may, from time to time also include spouses. In return for all of these actions he may get enhanced loyalty and greater efficiency from his work-force. Without these things, however, he is sure not to.

It is not at all a given that other countries in Asia, particularly those bordering on Singapore, will follow the island state in all of its employee behavioural characteristics, but some signs are already there and need to be closely monitored and controlled. Theoretically in Malaysia, unemployment will go negative by the year 2000 and the country will be short of at least half a million workers. As quality and distribution of labour throughout Malaysia is by no means perfect, this has already translated into acute shortages in various employment categories, most particularly technical and engineering positions creating some of the attendant woes currently being experienced by Singapore.

Other results of full employment, improved education and a more vocal work-force include social unrest and labour unionisation. This was unfortunately most visible in Thailand in 1992 and has created an on-going wariness in investors in that country, most especially amongst the Japanese. The number of industrial strikes occurring during the past two years in Thailand and Hong Kong have dramatically increased and is being mirrored elsewhere throughout the Asian region as demands for improved treatment of and benefits to employees, hitherto not very vocal, are beginning to be aired. Human Resources managers over the next decade in Asia would be well advised to ensure they are one step ahead of their increasingly well-educated work-force demands or they may find themselves with yet another major managerial problem to solve.

CHAPTER 9
THE HEARTBEAT OF THE COMPANY

"How's it going down there?" barked the big walrus from his perch on the highest rock near the shore. He waited for the good word. Down below the smaller walruses conferred hastily among themselves. Things were not going well at all, but none of them wanted to break the news to the Old Man. He was the biggest and wisest walrus in the herd, and he knew his business - but he did hate to hear bad news. And he had such a terrible temper that every walrus in the herd was terrified of his ferocious bark.

"What will we tell him?" whispered Basil, the second ranking walrus. He well remembered how the Old Man had raved and ranted at him the last time the herd caught less than its quota of herring and he had no desire to go through that experience again. Nevertheless, the walruses had noticed for several weeks that the water level in the nearby Arctic bay had been falling constantly and it had become necessary to travel much further to catch the dwindling supply of herring. Someone should tell the Old Man; he would probably know what to do. But who? And how?

Finally, Basil spoke up, "Things are going pretty well Chief," he said. The thought of the receding waterline made his heart feel heavy, but he went on, "As a matter of fact, the beach seems to be getting larger. The Old Man grunted, "Fine, fine" he said, "That will give us a bit more elbow room."

He closed his eyes and continued basking in the sun.

The next day brought more trouble. A new herd of walruses moved in down the beach and with the supply of herring dwindling, this invasion could be dangerous. No one wanted to tell the Old Man, though only he could take the steps necessary to meet this new competition. Reluctantly, Basil approached the big walrus, who was still sunning himself on the large rock. After some small talk, he said, "Oh, by the way, Chief, a new herd of walruses seems to have moved into our territory."

The Old Man's eyes snapped open and he filled his great lungs in preparation for a mighty bellow. But Basil added quickly, "Of course we don't anticipate any trouble. They don't look like herring eaters to me - more likely interested in minnows and, as you know, we don't

54

bother with minnows ourselves."

The Old Man let out the air with a long sigh. "Good, good," he said, "No point in our getting excited over nothing, is there?"

Things didn't get any better in the weeks that followed.

One day, peering down from the large rock, the Old Man noticed that part of his herd seemed to be missing. Summoning Basil, he grunted peevishly, "What's going on, Basil, where is everybody?"

Poor Basil didn't have the courage to tell the Old Man that many of the younger walruses were leaving every day to join the new herd. Clearing his throat nervously, he said, "Well, Chief we've been tightening things up a bit. You know, getting rid of some of the dead wood. After all, a herd is only as good as the walruses in it."

"Run a tight ship, I always say," the Old Man grunted. "Glad to hear that everything's going so well."

Before long, everyone but Basil had left to join the new herd. Basil realised that the time had come to tell the Old Man the facts. Terrified but determined , he flopped up to the huge rock. "Chief," he said, "I have bad news. The rest of the herd has left you."

The old walrus was so astonished that he couldn't even work up a good bellow, "Left me!" he cried. "All of them ; but why? How could this happen? I can't understand it," the old walrus said, "And just when everything was going so well."

(From "Management Review" 1961 "The fable of the ill-informed walrus")

In the position description of every Human Resources Manager should be words such as "responsible for feeling the pulse of the company" and this is what he or she must do. It is a primary role for Human Resources practitioners in Asia but few fulfil the role. This lack of fulfilment arises from a number of different and diverse reasons. Some relate to the 'excuse' of insufficient time available to stop and chat with the workforce and its supervisors due to the heavy workload of the day. Others are a little less palatable to accept, such as the Human Resources Managers who now believe that because of their elevated status, mixing with the workforce is just a little below them and is a more suitable task to be performed by the more junior officer in the department. Whatever the reasons, the Human Resources Manager is not fulfilling the role for which he or she is being employed unless they are "out there" constantly feeling the pulse of their organisation and ensuring that the top management of the company does not suddenly wake up to some unpleasant surprises.

Human Resources Managers must be fully aware of rumblings for unionisation, dissatisfaction with a particular policy or manager's style in order that they may rapidly jump in and diffuse the problem. Regrettably, the HR profession in Asia is not yet, in general, as well respected and progressed as it is in other parts of the developed world, most particularly in the USA and Europe. Accordingly, it is less recognised that the Human Resources Manager has either this part to play or the necessary authority to carry it through. The situation will change but gradually and will not be assisted in some cultures, most notably, Japanese, Korean and Chinese where such behaviour by the HR Manager could be seen to be counter productive and confusing to the company's hierarchical relationships.

Not only feeling the pulse but also being the heartbeat is a role to be performed by the Human Resources Manager. Being the heartbeat ensures that he or she creates activities especially of a healthy motivational nature for the workforce and management of the company to enjoy together. He or she must ensure that all the body parts of the organisation are functioning well by providing life-blood to every limb and vessel, whether near or remote and by ensuring that each receives its fair and continuous share.

Fear and distrust must be driven from the workplace and it is the responsibility of the HR practitioner to be aware of where it exists and how to remove it. For, if it remains unchecked it will create a decline in motivation and commitment from the workforce. Fear stems from insecurity and instability, from managers who are always looking for problem areas and then making capital from them rather than searching for occasions and for examples of employees performing their tasks well and deserving complimentary remarks and consequent re-affirmation of their value to the company.

Costs in low morale, high turnover and negative attitudes of the workforce can be very high and often translate into poor quality products and service. It is for the HR manager to be aware when fear exists in the organisation and to tutor managers guilty of creating that fear into more positive work habits where trust features prominently and where mistakes are understood to be an acceptable part of the learning process. We would do well to remember the story of when the founder of IBM who, on being approached by a young manager whose error had just cost the company millions and consequently felt obliged to offer his resignation replied by saying, "What! Let you go, and I've just spent ten million dollars on your training and education - not likely - get on with the job."

Such are the leadership stories to inspire and create loyalty from employees. Fear should have no place in a company. Fear does not inspire people to improved consistency in results. Rather, the qualities in the organisation which should be constantly sought after and encouraged by the CEO and the Human Resources Manager, providing a healthy heart and pulse are those of high ethical standards of management, this being the real cornerstone of success of any enterprise. In addition, enthusiasm is a most valuable asset but the correct environment must be generated to ensure that real enthusiasm has time and place in which to develop. A high energy level should be on display especially from all supervisory and managerial staff. Courage in decision making, risk taking and holding individualistic views is much to be admired in any company and within any manager who must also have the ability to set and to work on priorities and the patience to help others grow. All of these attributes and others are displayed in the values and enacted in the daily working styles of the most successful companies in Asia and, by virtue of the Human Resources Manager leading the way in continually ensuring that this healthy pulse beats strongly, these companies will retain their competitive edge.

People should be encouraged to create the future of the company and consequently, their own. Managers who prune their staff excessively in the hope of bringing in people with higher enthusiasm than they perceive in their existing staff should look first to their own practices. When they have problems at home with their children they do not send them away and get new ones. Rather they cajole, encourage, assist and eventually improve, in the main, wayward behaviour. So it is with our staff in our companies. Most people are worth developing and want to be developed. It is up to the leader to create and sustain an environment in which such development can occur.

To some extent it boils down to the acceptance of personality. A person's adaptive personality can be changed but a person's core personality cannot. It is very motivating if a person can accept and be accepted as his or her core personality dictates. Forcing a person into a role at work which reacts against his or her core personality is a recipe for failure. We tend to recruit people who are like ourselves, who possess similar values to our own. Rather, we should recruit complimentary and competitive personnel and accept their personality strengths and weaknesses and maximise their utility for the organisation. It is also important to have humour in the workplace and space for people to vent their emotions. If there is no safe place to vent emotions then underlying alliances and office politics begin and become destructive forces within the company. The Human Resources specialist has to become the "heart" of the company, the facilitator nurturing a positive behaviour within the company.

The Human Resources Manager has to be an excellent and professional listener. Most people do not listen with the intent to understand, they listen with the intent to reply. Listening with the intention of understanding is an acquired skill but one that the HR Manager must develop if he or she really hopes to be able to feel the pulse of the organisation. An article written in 1952 in the Harvard Business Review is as vibrant and appropriate today as it was more than forty years ago. The authors, Carl Rogers and F.J. Roethlisberger argued that "the best way to test the quality of your understanding the next time you get into an argument with your spouse, friend, work group or manager is to stop the discussion for a moment and suggest this rule. Before each person speaks up, he or she must *first* restate the ideas and feelings of the previous speaker accurately and to that speaker's satisfaction."

You see what this would mean? Before presenting your own point of view, you would first have to achieve the other speaker's frame of reference. Sounds simple, doesn't it? But, if you try it, you will find it one of the most difficult things you have ever attempted to do. And, even when you have been able to do it, your comments will have to be drastically revised. But you will also find that the emotion is dissipating - the differences are reduced and those that remain are rational and understandable. This sage advice was offered over forty years ago and we would be fooling ourselves to believe that the suggested technique will find an easy welcoming home in many Asian companies, but that should not stop us from, little by little, using these and other techniques to improve the atmosphere and environment in our companies so that our pulse beats even stronger.

CHAPTER 10
THE WESTERN EXPATRIATE

It could be argued that there are essentially three types of Western expatriate. The first is the in-company expatriate who, generally, has one spell of expatriation and can often see it as a necessary evil in terms of the development of his career. The second type is the expatriate who is truly mobile and willing to live almost anywhere as long as the job and the compensation are attractive to him. The remaining type is the third-country national who is very integrated into a specific country or region, does not wish to leave and to return to his home country and has excellent local business and cultural knowledge.

The 'ideal' expatriate is an adventurous person, willing to live anywhere and to learn the culture, habits and customs of the country and to accept local difficulties. A dependable person who is self-sufficient and strong enough to resist compromising situations. Most probably, married with a secure relationship and a spouse who enjoys adventure, travel and the life of an expatriate. Preferably a person who has an aptitude for language, certainly fluent in English, which is the business language of Asia and dedicated to learning the language of his new country. He or she is a committed expatriate, happy to be so for the major part, if not the entirety, of their careers. This expatriate is a flexible person, willing to live in "difficult" as well as easy conditions and to accept that children will probably have to be educated in their home country. Both husband and wife are interesting people with hobbies that allow them to be able to quickly relax in their new environment and to integrate better into the new country.

Costs associated with supporting expatriates have to be minimised and most companies are either looking at localisation of expatriate positions or, at least, at extending the expatriation period. This is because most expatriation postings are less than five years which means that the "set up" and "return" costs occur frequently. If expatriates remain in their host country longer than five years, learning and acclimatisation has a real opportunity to be beneficial to themselves and to their performance in their jobs and they are not looking for their next move and "positioning" themselves for it after only two or three years of the posting. Many companies spend insufficient time understanding and explaining the affects of culture shock and its stages and remedies, especially to first-time expatriates to Asia. Studies clearly demonstrate that any expatriation goes through the following stages; euphoria at the idea of expatriation, especially to a new and exotic country, this soon to be followed by deflation at the reality of day to day life dealing with the difficulties and differences of the new country and, for Westerners in Asia, the distance from home and families. Then there grows a competence as daily tasks become easier with familiarity and as a network of friends is gradually created. The final stage is one of adaptation and a feeling of ease and enjoyment of the new lifestyle.

Some expatriates never make it beyond level two. In such a situation it is invariably preferable to ship them home no matter how "essential" they are to the project, for their attitudes will negatively affect their new colleagues and the success of the project. They are also likely to bad mouth to ex-colleagues back at headquarters, the expatriate situation, creating real difficulties in encouraging new expatriates to that country or project. Some symptoms to look for which display an inability of the expatriate or his spouse to move beyond level two include, excessive washing of hands and concern over drinking water, food, dishes and bedding or a fear of physical contact with the new environment which can often result in reclusive and solitary drinking habits. Other signs are feelings of helplessness and a desire for dependence upon long-term residents of their own nationality rather than cultivating friendships with newer expatriates. An outright refusal to learn the language of the host country and fits of unreasonable anger over delays and other minor irritations are further indications of an inability to cope as is, of course, a terrible longing to be back in the home country. Companies should advise senior managers on signs to look for in their expatriates at the work place which show early warning signals of stress, worry and inability to cope. These include frequent and unexplained absences, sickness, poor time keeping, moodiness, irritability, lethargy, deterioration in relationships, reluctance to accept responsibility and untidiness in dress habits. A study done in Guy's hospital London, showed that the normal sequence of events that affect the "collapse" of an expatriate are firstly poor work followed by family and marital problems, an over dependence upon alcohol, increasing psychosomatic illnesses followed, in the more extreme cases, by a complete psychological breakdown. Some companies feel it wise to provide psychometric testing for the proposed expatriate and spouse prior to the final decision on expatriation.

The recognition of the power of the expatriate wife on the success or otherwise of the expatriation, especially in some of the more difficult locations in Asia is now quite well appreciated. Gone are the "good old days" of the simple appointment of the lucky executive destined for the top, or pretty near, as long as he does his spell in the backwoods of the corporate empire and drags along his chattels of wife and belongings with him. Today the company has to care, to really care, about his wife, her feelings and her performance as an expatriate. In fact, her performance and success can often be a more critical factor than that of the employee. If she is successful and happy, content to live in the company-imposed alien environment, lacking the recognised comforts of home, then the success of the expatriation is largely secured. Many corporations spend vast amounts of financial resources on equipping their employees technologically and managerially to perform their designated roles in the farther flung outposts of the corporate empire only to have that expense evaporate meaninglessly as they are forced to repatriate the disenchanted family due to domestic tension or crisis. The more enlightened companies avoid such a trauma and expense by employing, from the outset, a meaningful family expatriation policy.

Such a policy would include a selection process involving a joint interview with both candidate and spouse, an introduction of the real situation to be found in the host country involving videos of the good and bad aspects and an open discussion with previous expatriates having returned or currently residing in the proposed host country.

Schooling requirements should be comprehensively researched and all difficulties faced. The issue of spouse employment in the host country must be considered, especially in a situation where that spouse is currently following a meaningful career in the home country. Should compensation for the loss of the spouse's employment be considered, especially in the situation where he or she will find it difficult, if not impossible, to follow that career in Asia?

For a company to blindly proceed in the expatriation with insufficiently determined answers to the problems of the spouse and children spells potential disaster for that expatriation. Further, reports of one disaster can often create increasing difficulty at head office to find the next expatriate for that location. If acceptable solutions at the detailed pre-appointment screening stage cannot be determined, then the expatriation should not proceed. An alternative candidate must be found, for if not, the consequent costs in financial and human terms of an unsatisfactory expatriation will far outweigh any benefits gained.

Once the potential expatriate and spouse have been determined, pre-expatriation acclimatisation should occur. This obviously varies dependent upon the extent of differences in culture, climate and customs from the home to the host country. An expatriation from France to Spain or from England to America has fewer dramatic differences than that of an expatriation from Brussels to Bangkok. The common business language of Asia is English. If the expatriate, spouse and children do not have a good command of this language then it is the company's responsibility to provide this training, as intensively as possible, prior to the expatriation. It should be self-evident that if the company employee does not have a good command of English then he or she should not be sent to Asia for there will be insufficient time to develop the necessary proficiency and the efficiency of the business will suffer.

The difficulty of living and doing business in another country is illustrated by the high expatriate failure rate. In London, the rate is 18%, as reported by the Business Council for International Understanding. In Tokyo, the failure rate is 36%. As each failure can cost the company anything from $250,000 to $1 million, it is vital that as full a preparation and as comprehensive a support mechanism as possible is afforded the expatriate, especially first timers. It is for this reason that many companies would rather recruit local staff even if they are regarded as a little less competent than the well-known employee from head office. Another solution is to recruit the well tried and tested Western expatriate already resident in Asia and to teach him or her the necessary company skills or culture. It is time to accept the difficulty of describing a company as global in a context in which only 7% of American senior management can speak a foreign language or have had any inter cultural experience, this 7% reducing to an insignificant number if only Asian expatriate postings are considered.

But some companies can seem to get it right constantly. How do they do it? Generally they are companies whose home base is in a very small country providing less than 10% of their turnover and they have been forced for growth into the international market place. This has created a situation where expatriation becomes a norm for the executives of the company rather than an experience limited to a chosen few. Recruits to these companies realise even before they are employed, that their future lies in expatriation and they consequently already have a positive mind set to the situation. Indeed, their personalities are such that they already possess many of the attributes of the "ideal" expatriate. It is also true to say that they have grown up in a country culture where expatriation is the norm and commonplace amongst school friends and business associates. Some of the best examples of such types come from the countries of England and Holland.

In Philips, expatriate positions, particularly in the larger subsidiaries, have been very attractive for their managers for a variety of reasons. With only 7% or 8% of its total sales coming from Holland, many different national subsidiaries of the company have contributed much larger shares of total revenues than the parent company. As a result, foreign operations have enjoyed relatively high organisational status compared to most companies of similar size with headquarters in the United States, Japan or even the larger countries in Europe. Further, because of the importance of its foreign operations, Philips' formal management development system has always required considerable international experience as a prerequisite for top corporate positions. Collectively, these factors have led to the best and brightest of Phillips managers spending much of their careers in different national operations. Unlike many other European and Japanese companies where an expatriate manager typically spends a tour of duty of three to six years in a particular national subsidiary and then returns to the headquarters, expatriate managers in Philips spend a large part of their careers abroad continuously working for two or three years each in a number of different subsidiaries. This difference in the career systems results in very different attitudes. In Philips, the expatriate managers follow each other into assignments and build close relationships among themselves. Being much more internationalised than their counterparts from other companies, they are much less likely to take a custodial approach which resists any local changes to standard products and policies and are more willing to be advocates of local views and to defend against the imposition of inappropriate corporate ideas on national organisations. By creating this kind of environment in the national organisations, Philips has less difficulty than its counterparts in attracting and retaining very capable local management.

Some companies have gone to the stage of creating or considering creating an "expatriate battalion" which is a group of mobile professional employees whose entire career, from recruitment, is accepted as being an expatriate one. Consequently, the chances are that they will remain highly motivated no matter where they are sent in the world and recognise that their compensation is appropriate whether they happen to be this year in Korea or next year in Bangkok. Having such a flexible group of people allows company growth opportunities to be planned and structured in the knowledge that key personnel, the shortage of which is often a limiting factor to growth, will be readily available and that the search for willing and competent personnel for overseas assignments inside and outside the company is minimised. The careers of members of an "expatriate battalion" should be well managed and care should be taken to ensure that their future possibilities compare favourably with those individuals remaining constantly in the home country. This can mean that a national manager accepts that each year he or she will have an allocation of members from the "battalion" working in their country. It is important to retain these expatriates as expatriates rather than bringing them home even in situations where there is no overseas work available to them, as interrupting the cycle can result in complicated procedures of stopping and starting. Group identity is important and can be nurtured by having a senior company individual or even board member dedicated to the management of the group with the responsibility of not only understanding and tracking the development of the company employee but also that of the spouse and family. Sensitivity to potential jealousies amongst non-expatriates is essential, but a precise answer is available, "apply to become a member of the battalion, - but be sure that you are willing to commit to twenty years as an expatriate."

But the world of the Western expatriate in Asia has entered a period of dramatic change. A short time ago almost anywhere in Asia, the Western expatriate could demand hardship posting allowance, car with driver, well situated and maintained housing complete with amenities, often including a swimming pool and at least one Amah to manage the household whilst his wife hurried about on her round of social events. His children would be educated at no cost to himself in the best local schools or back in the home country and his family would have free passage, at least once per year to escape from their expatriation difficulties returning for refreshment to the comfort of home where they would recharge their batteries and complain about their problems during at least one month of every year.

Today, the world has changed. Asian countries and companies operating in Asia have far fewer requirements for expatriates than they had last year, which was less than the year before, which was less than the year before that. Educated Asians are now commonly seen in the top positions of Western multinational companies competently developing their company's prosperity throughout the Asian region. Knowledge and experience of the company corporate culture is necessary for these managers, but that can be given to them at a fraction of the cost of the Western expatriate's package. So where does that leave our Western expatriate of today? Probably in one of four places.

Firstly, within one of the relatively few Western companies or perhaps, banks, who still feel that they must have the technological competence and company knowledge which comes only from staff sent out to Asia from head office. This is a fast dwindling number and one in danger of eventual extinction within ten years.

Secondly, the Western expatriate may find himself back in Europe or America and often disadvantaged in terms of competing for promotional possibilities as the corporate world and his peers have not stood still in his absence. Certainly, he has a good experience of Asia but, do we really need that back at headquarters? We now have "a real" Asian at the helm and it is his show anyway. Such expatriates often find that the disillusionment of return forces them away from their current employment or even back to Asia, which they know and have come to love. Following this disillusionment, these people are frequently willing to accept the return under "local" conditions.

Thirdly, is the Western expatriate who remains under a localisation agreement which essentially gives him or her a compensation package equivalent to that of the local Asian manager performing a similar role. All the hitherto attractive benefits of expatriation, house, car, education and so on - being relinquished for the chance of living and working in a high growth environment generally with a very positive work ethic and in a climate far preferable to the cold and wet of home. Such managers, once they have passed through the difficult transitional first year or so of loss of expatriation benefits and becoming localised, still realise and accept that their quality of life remains superior to that which they could reasonably expect to achieve in their home countries.

The fourth avenue for the non-returning expatriate becoming local is within the consultancy profession where he or she can bring much needed and balanced expertise to rapidly growing and sometimes unstructured companies, especially in countries such as Indonesia where today, the most sought after individuals in business are company "doctors" and management consultants. Although difficult to get started in this profession, unless one were to join a well established consultancy firm, it can be a most exciting and rewarding activity for a mature Western manager who can really bring meaningful added-value, albeit on a temporary basis, to fast developing locally run Asian companies.

As more and more ex-expatriates become localised in the countries of Asia, they can, if the local environment is an accepting one, bring expertise to the community in which they live. Expertise which goes well beyond business requirements. They can assist and bring different perspectives and knowledge to social, quasi-political and community development projects. These are areas in which their spouses can also develop a most meaningful role. Integration may never be total but both parties benefit from an open acceptance and local community life can often be materially enhanced.

CHAPTER 11
IS YOUR HUMAN RESOURCE
SPECIALIST A BUSINESSMAN?

To be truly effective, your Human Resource specialist must be "the Businessman responsible for Human Resources." He differs from the businessman responsible for Sales and Marketing or the Businessman responsible for General Management only in the skills he has and the tools he uses.

However, unlike the Sales and Marketing businessman or the Financial specialist, both of whom can successfully live their lives and expand their careers in their chosen discipline, the Human Resources Specialist cannot hope to be a successful professional unless he is a convincing all-rounder. If he has not performed roles in, especially, plant management or had bottom line responsibility for a commercial operation, he cannot expect to be credible to his colleagues.

Although Human Resource associations in every country do fine work in their specific domain and within their geographical boundaries, they often fail to recognise and advise their budding students and younger members that to really succeed in Human Resources work, they must leave this chosen career for at least ten years in order to follow different paths and to experience different business disciplines. The Human Resource specialist must swing from branch to branch of the corporate tree whilst his colleagues climb steadily upwards or crawl consistently along the same branch.

The responsibility of the Human Resources Specialist is both to manage and advise how to manage, the most volatile and expensive asset of your business. He has to be as competent as your best engineering analyst in ensuring the "machinery" works in a total quality fashion and that both planned maintenance and emergency repairs are equally possible. He has to fight to ensure that these assets are purchased at the right cost, perform satisfactorily, are well-oiled and provide the right quality end product. He has also to ensure that when their useful life is completed, they are disposed of in an environmentally friendly fashion. Let us take a couple of examples, - Monday morning brings the Sales Manager to the Human Resources Specialist's door. He has in his hand the required requisition form, signed by the General Manager and authorising the request for a new

Area Sales Executive. He informs the Human Resources Manager that the need for the addition is both vital and immediate. The General Manager concurs. "So, HR Department, do your job, get me the right person tomorrow !"

Ninety per cent of Human Resources departments will now swing into action, place advertisements, telephone the executive search companies, do whatever they consider necessary to recruit the new Area Sales Executive. - Let us look at the ten per cent who have not behaved so incautiously. They are the ten per cent who have been outside the HR function for many years and even, perhaps, been in the Sales Manager or General Manager position but now have the advantage over both in that they are not pressurised by the daily or monthly need to reach the sales targets imposed. They can take a longer and more demanding view. This ten per cent request a discussion on total organisation of the sales department. Could reorganisation result in re-allocation of jobs so that the need for a new Area Sales Executive recedes? They ask for the five year plan of the Sales department or help the Sales Manager to create one. They ask for sales turnover statistics by area, they request profitability per salesman. They look, together with the Sales manager, at the performance reviews of existing sales and other non-sales departmental staff ensuring that an internal candidate is not missed. They look at other departments and divisions of the company. They work out reallocation of tasks and jobs within the division, within the company. They regard the expenditure of $100,000 that the new person will cost as if it were coming out of their own pockets. Then and only when all else fails, do they agree to recruit for the new position.

It is interesting to note that following such an analysis, it is often necessary to action probably only half of such requests made and it is so much more satisfactory to show that objectives have been met in turnover, profitability and enhanced morale by an internal solution to the activity proposed than to have had the expense and the trauma of going outside the company and bringing in an "unknown" . The Human Resources specialist has calmed the situation down, looked at longer term bottom line contribution from the proposed new position and, because he has been "in the chair" himself, has both the credibility and experience to be able to question deeply the request of the Sales Manager. More often than not, the Sales Manager goes away satisfied with the solution and hopefully, next time, not so prone to immediately failing into a crisis management mode. The Human Resources Manager would not have been legitimately able to question the Sales Manager or to demand the information and to process the questioning in the way he did unless he had the personal credibility of having himself been in an equivalent position to that of the Sales Manager at some stage in his career.

To take another example, Friday morning. The Plant Manager looking grim comes to inform the Human Resources specialist that due to decreasing demand, he has to remove ten per cent of his workforce. "Please action, Mr HR specialist, I'll send the people to you. We'll choose on the basis of " last in first out."

"Not so fast," says the ten per cent of the HR function. Not so fast. Let us look at orders in house, inventory levels, are these areas we can save substantial amounts of money before we have to begin impacting peoples' jobs and affecting the standing of our image in the local community? Where are we on the business cycle? Have we already peaked for the year and all is now downhill or are we in reality just at the beginning of the cycle and having an unusually bad first quarter because one of our major customers has a temporary problem? What is our current profitability by product line? Not just at the gross margin level but also at operating margin? Are we backing the wrong product horses inadvertently? What are the costs of continuing to manufacture and store versus the costs, both in terms of dollars and cents and in terms of morale, of laying off people? The latter question is of primary importance for a company new to an Asian market and new can easily mean having been there for less than five to seven years. An image as an unreliable employer can linger a very long time indeed in many of the countries and cultures of Asia. Much more so than it would do in the USA or in Europe. Let us visit the R and D Department and Production Engineering to see which products they could conceivably bring to production faster if they altered their focus or had a few more competent hands and minds from the production unit to assist them. Let us analyse with Finance all the costs of manufacture, as labour, being often no more than thirty per cent of standard cost and often much less, could be the last cost area to attack rather than the first. Let us look at the possible reorganisation of manufacturing overheads. Are they currently and meaningfully classified today or is it time for us to take a fundamental look at the way our organisation is structured and determine its appropriateness both for today and for the next decade. The current hiatus should force us to address these fundamental questions rather than remaining in grim acceptance of the inevitable status quo. Let us meet with the Sales Director to determine whether we can sell our way out of the situation. Can labour from the plant be put to work and become more of a direct sales supporting activity? Let us talk to our suppliers to extend further our lead times or payment terms. Will the work force agree to a temporary reduction in income to save the jobs of colleagues? Is job sharing a possibility? - In other words, let us not simply accept the situation. For in this acceptance there may not only be a major human resources problem today but also another in months to come as the business again turns around.

Intrinsically, the Plant Manager or the Finance Manager may believe there could be a more acceptable resolution to the problem but there is much pressure upon them to act quickly and decisively. Only the HR businessman can refuse to accept their solution to the problem until and unless all other avenues are fully explored. But he can only do this well if they know he has been "in the chair" and really understands the composition of standard cost of manufacture, inventory, purchasing and stock holding and financing methods and the necessity or not of supporting certain overhead functions and the legitimate short cuts that can be made to bring product on to the factory floor more quickly. This understanding being further enhanced by employing a variety of possible sales solutions that he may himself have attempted in the past. This HR businessman is a credible arguer of the situation rather than sitting in passive acceptance or frustrated non acceptance. In his credible arguments and, hopefully, improved resolution to the problem, employee morale and company image is sustained. So, how do we find such a person? There are not too many available in Asia today. Companies have not historically regarded the Human Resources function as a full fledged business division of their company and consequently have ill-prepared the incumbents in such roles. The HR businessman has to be developed but it is obviously a long term activity. The primary mover, certainly in the present development status of the function and its recognition, is the career HR specialist himself. He or she must really want to be a businessman. They must force themselves, careerwise, into different disciplines. If the company does not wish to assist in this process, then a change in companies is called for. Perhaps even, for a while, the HR specialist will have to go into business for himself or herself or assist in the management of a family business. The budding HR businessman has to push, push, push to create the opportunities that will offer the essential experience.

Companies must begin to recognise their responsibility in offering support and opportunity to the young human resources professional to develop his or her career outside the more obvious areas of specialism and qualification and to take a long term pragmatic view. The short cuts many companies take by recruiting a life-long HR specialist and expecting him to operate meaningfully as a contributor to overall business strategy or working in advisory roles to the other senior departmental managers of the company is just as likely to be as unsuccessful as taking a seasoned and successful marketing manager and putting him in charge of the Human Resources activity. The blinkered career HR specialist cannot hope to be credible when he tries to advise outside the immediate skills he has received in his education and experience. The seasoned businessman usually does not possess the techniques, technical skills and people awareness dynamics which would equip him to perform well in the HR role.

There are two prime movers charged with the responsibility for upgrading the awareness and professionalism of the Human Resources function, the HR professional and his or her company. Together they must develop a businessmen for, unless your Human Resources specialist is "The businessman responsible for Human Resources", you have second best and your company will not be performing in the most efficient way and utilising its human resources in the most profitable fashion.

Having reached the situation where the Human Resources professional is respected as a businessman, it is now essential that he or she creates within the organisation an awareness and belief that the Human Resources department is a profit centre and not an expense overhead department clothed in mystique. The HR professional needs to convince all levels of management that the HR policies and activities are major contributors to the growth and wealth of the company. The HR case must be presented in dollars and cents rather than in procedures and systems. If a position evaluation structure is being proposed to the company, it needs to be presented in the light of how it will improve efficiency, reduce cost or improve profitability.

As a project, it should be able to stand stringent financial analysis just in the same way as when the engineering department suggests the purchase of new tooling or machinery and the pay back and efficiency gains such a purchase would occasion. Human Resources is not a welfare function employing people to do good deeds. It is there to make money. There are some difficulties in measuring the cost of poor morale, of inefficient pay scales and of high turnover, but, given a little latitude, anything can be measured. No Human Resources policy should be offered to a company unless it is accompanied by a cost and income analysis to support it.

Managers have to be convinced that the Human Resources Department is providing a necessary product and is doing so cost-efficiently. Further, the HR activity must be seen as being of key strategic importance to the development of every department and to the company as a whole. It must be seen as a real management function, staffed by high quality personnel who come from an excellent all-round business base experience so that they can talk with authority and implement with credibility.

72

CHAPTER 12
THE HUMAN RESOURCES LOOP

The influences that are brought to bear on the formulation and enactment of a Human Resources policy in a company in Asia are many and varied, but the major influences include:-

Economic - What can the company afford to do? How competitive does it want to be? What is the people related cost in a particular location or country?

Political - How stable is the workforce and the environment in which the company operates?

Social - What are the demographics of the workforce; ageing or young? What are the expectations of the workforce and how good a "social citizen " does the company want to be?

Legislation - What is the legal framework under which the company has to work? Can we accept it?

Company plans - Investment plans, expansion or retrenchment concerns. Will the workforce, especially key managerial employees be available? If not, what to do?

Company culture - What type of people fit in and which do not ? Do we want to change the culture and to do so by attracting different types of employee than is the norm today?

Country or regional culture - How acceptable is it? How able are we to cope with it? Some cultures, often Western, view man as the master of nature which can be harnessed and exploited to suit man's needs. Time, change and uncertainty can be actively managed. Truth is determined by facts and measurement. Other cultures, often Eastern, view man as subservient to or in harmony with nature. Time, change and uncertainty are accepted as given. "Truth" is determined by spiritual and philosophical principles. This attitude is often referred to as "fatalistic" or "adaptive. "

There are certain assumptions underlying Human Resource management practices which have to be questioned concerning their fit within different national cultures. Special attention must be paid to Human Resources management practices such as career planning, performance management, appraisals and reward systems, selection, socialisation and expatriate assignments.

Assumptions regarding the nature of human relationships are also different. The importance of social concerns over task, of the hierarchy and of the individual versus the group are clearly different not only between the East and the West but also within Eastern and Western cultures themselves. In Eastern cultures, for example, importance is placed on social versus task concerns, on the hierarchy and on the group. By contrast, in Western cultures, the focus is more on task, on the individual and the hierarchy is considered to be of less importance.

These differences have implications for human resources policies that are developed at headquarters and that reflect not only the corporate culture but also the national culture of the multi-national corporation. Problems may arise when these policies are to be implemented abroad, especially if insufficient cognisance is made of local conditions and culture. Multi-national corporations can choose from a "menu" of human resources practices that concern staffing, appraising, compensating, selection and socialising. Within this menu there are several options which need to be in line with the overall corporate strategy and culture. They also need to take into account the differences in the national cultures of the subsidiaries where they are to be implemented.

As people make things happen and as we should regard them as investments or added value contributors rather than costs, we should expect to measure the worth of an organisation by the quality and contribution of its human resources. The corporate board of most large companies should essentially have two tasks; major investment and strategic decision making on the one hand and the management of human resources on the other. The corporate culture should be driven by this board to ensure that excellent environmental working conditions exist which include the provision of immediate, personal, business and development counselling which is both welcomed and confidential.

Induction is a process, not a short programme. It is a very critical but often missed or abbreviated step. The very minimum we should do is to spend one day with each new employee ensuring that they are knowledgeable about the company, who they are working with, what is expected of them and who they can go to for assistance. The provision of a "buddy" assists dramatically in this process. If new employees are not well introduced into their company, despite their desire to perform well, their motivation will be reduced and they will probably perform below their maximum ability as they spend wasteful time trying to find their way around. Similarly, it is vital that we establish the boundaries of responsibility with the new employee and ensure that they do not simply float along, never quite knowing what is expected of them. The management of objectives provides a focus for the activities of the employee and helps to remove subjectivity from the performance management and appraisal system. Performance cannot be successfully measured unless there has been some form of prior objective or task setting, and this should be done in such a way that both parties regard it as, in a non-legalistic way, a contract to be fulfilled and to have regular points, throughout the year, when assistance can be given to ensure that the contract is being complied with. It is important in this process to imbibe as much personal responsibility and authority within the employee as possible. This may mean that we, as managers, may have to give up some of our control, de-emphasising the power we have over people under us and acknowledge that while the captain may choose direction, the engine room drives the ship. The performance review or appraisal process should hold no surprises as there has been continual dialogue between subordinate and supervisor. It is extremely important, even in the cultures of Asia, to stress performance. This is partly because of the vibrant business environment and partly because the workforce is comparatively youthful requiring much guidance.

Employee motivational and empowerment programmes are not a fad, they will not go away. Companies have to take a fundamental look at their corporate culture and alter their behaviour in order to ensure they are producing the most appropriate and challenging environment possible to be able to attract the best of the scarce supply of managerial talent in Asia. Every company must have competitive salaries and benefits which often derive from structured modern job evaluation schemes leading to ensuring equitability in internal relativities and a real ability to compare logically with the external market place. Moreover, job evaluation drives to some degree a job description which ensures greater understanding by employees of their jobs, performance expectations and a rationalised reward system.

Management development and succession planning can be viewed at two levels. That which is planned strictly within Asia and that which includes the world of the company. Indeed, international management development, despite its complexity and its time-consuming problems, is the crux of Human Resource management in the multi-national enterprise. It is the responsibility of HR departments in Asia to provide a meaningful management development programme for executives in Asia and to build, ever increasingly, local expertise to a level which allows the minimum necessity for expatriation. As many operations in Asia are of a joint venture nature, it makes the localisation of expatriate positions even more difficult. However, there is always a time when the future arrives and if we do not successfully plan for it well in advance we will be caught unprepared and unable to take full advantage of the business opportunity being offered to us.

Human Resource management is still in its infancy as a formal management tool within companies in Asia. Until recently most companies tended towards reactive "crisis management" of their human resources. Human Resource management can never be an exact or predictable activity because we are dealing with individuals, all of whom are unique. But we recognise we must give careful attention to our human resource planning and processes. Such strategies must support the strategic planning of the company as a whole, since without the right people in the right places at the right time, the long term goals of the company cannot be achieved. There are three major objectives of a Human Resources department - attract, motivate, retain. All to be achieved by working with the managers and supervisors of each department who really are the ones that make these objectives successful.

SOURCE REFERENCES USED

BUSINESS ASIA

CORPORATE RESOURCES GROUP

EMPLOYMENT CONDITIONS ABROAD LTD

ECONOMIST INTELLIGENCE UNIT

HARVARD BUSINESS REVIEW

MANAGEMENT REVIEW

PACRIM

THE CUSTOMER COMES SECOND - ROSENBLUTH

S. SCHNEIDER - INSEAD